Editor
Sara Connolly

Editor in Chief
Brent L. Fox, M. Ed.

Creative Director
Sarah M. Fournier

Cover Artist
Diem Pascarella

Illustrators
Crystal-Dawn Keitz
Renée McElwee

Art Coordinator
Renée Mc Elwee

Imaging
Amanda R. Harter

Publisher
Mary D. Smith, M.S. Ed.

For standards correlations, visit
http://www.teachercreated.com/standards/.

Grades

TCR 8314

What Would YOU Do?

Exploring Difficult Decisions and Considering Consequences

- Realistic stories help children connect to experiences in their own lives

- Discussion and written questions provide opportunities for greater understanding

- Includes tips and strategies to improve social-emotional skills

- Helps children identify their emotions and the emotions of others

- Assists children in understanding the power of making choices

Teacher Created Resources

Author
Christina Hill, M.A.

Teacher Created Resources
12621 Western Avenue
Garden Grove, CA 92841
www.teachercreated.com
ISBN: 978-1-4206-8314-1

© 2021 Teacher Created Resources
Made in U.S.A.

Teacher Created Resources

Table of Contents

Introduction 3

How to Use This Book 3

Dealing with Emotions 5

Emotions Chart 7

Strategies 8

Strategies Chart 10

Unit 1: Anger 11
Understanding the Emotion—Basketball for All—Making Choices—What Do You Think?—What Would You Do?

Unit 2: Happiness 17
Understanding the Emotion—Donating Happiness—Making Choices—What Do You Think?—What Would You Do?

Unit 3: Sadness 23
Understanding the Emotion—Homesick—Making Choices—What Do You Think?—What Would You Do?

Unit 4: Fear 29
Understanding the Emotion—The Confrontation—Making Choices—What Do You Think?—What Would You Do?

Unit 5: Frustration 35
Understanding the Emotion—The Group Project—Making Choices—What Do You Think?—What Would You Do?

Unit 6: Shyness 41
Understanding the Emotion—The New School—Making Choices—What Do You Think?—What Would You Do?

Unit 7: Jealousy 47
Understanding the Emotion—A New Family—Making Choices—What Do You Think?—What Would You Do?

Unit 8: Anxiety 53
Understanding the Emotion—Sixth-Grade Science Camp—Making Choices—What Do You Think?—What Would You Do?

Unit 9: Embarrassment 59
Understanding the Emotion—The Shopping Trip—Making Choices—What Do You Think?—What Would You Do?

Unit 10: Worry 65
Understanding the Emotion—Quarantine Days—Making Choices—What Do You Think?—What Would You Do?

Resources 71
Journal Templates—Bonus Posters

Introduction

Social-Emotional Learning (SEL) has become the new focus point in the world of education. But what exactly is it, and how do we teach it? SEL entails providing students with the necessary tools needed to help them manage their emotions and make good decisions. When students are self-aware, they know how to talk about their feelings. When they feel comfortable talking about emotions, they can build stronger and healthier relationships with others. Students are able to manage their emotions and in turn, regulate those big feelings in positive ways. Students who are emotionally perceptive can feel empathy for others. This empathy eventually expands their social awareness as they grow up. They will learn to appreciate and relate to others, regardless of cultural and background differences.

The ultimate and most significant goal of SEL is to teach students to make wise and responsible choices. Students will learn to consider ethics, risk, safety, and emotional health before making decisions. In the past, social-emotional learning tended to be either glossed over or never truly addressed. However, studies are showing the importance of learning social-emotional wellness and how it relates to students' future happiness and success.

One of the greatest benefits of social-emotional learning is knowing that you are teaching young children real-life skills that will help them become successful, emotionally healthy adults. They will learn to handle stress in constructive and healthy ways. Students will have a higher rate of lifelong happiness and success in their academics, careers, and relationships. Students who learn coping skills and strategies tend to have fewer behavioral problems in school and even less criminal behavior later in life. Social-emotional health equates to better lifelong mental health. Sounds beneficial, right? So now, let's learn how to successfully teach SEL!

How to Use This Book

This book provides tips and tools for strengthening your students' social-emotional learning (SEL) skills. Teaching SEL skills to students enables them to be successful adults. By providing them with coping strategies, they will be better equipped to manage and understand their own emotions and the emotions of others. Most importantly, students will learn how to make wise and healthy choices in a variety of difficult situations.

To begin, make a copy of the *Emotions Chart* (page 7) to share with students. Display the chart in your classroom so that students become familiar with the different emotions. The *Dealing with Emotions* section (pages 5–6) provides helpful guidelines for how to set up your classroom as a safe and comfortable place to openly discuss emotions. The *Strategies* section (pages 8–9) includes a variety of coping skills and ideas for teaching students how to deal with these big emotions. The *Strategies Chart* (page 10) is a practical sheet to display or distribute to students so they can have these strategies on hand.

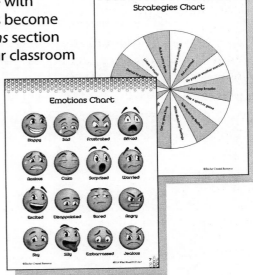

Introduction (cont.)

How to Use This Book (cont.)

There are ten units in this book. Each unit focuses on a different emotion: *anger, happiness, sadness, fear, frustration, shyness, jealousy, anxiety, embarrassment,* and *worry*. Every unit begins with a teacher page. This page will help you introduce the emotion to students. It contains supportive background information on each emotion and the physical responses that correlate. There is also a coping skill section that connects to the emotion being taught. Feel free to focus on this coping skill or use one of the strategies from the *Strategies Chart*.

Each unit's story is a leveled text that provides a scenario in which the main character is experiencing an emotion. Each story ends with a question: Should they do something or not? The next page gives two different endings to the story based on the answer that was chosen. This is followed by a page containing discussion questions for each ending.

There are a variety of ways to teach these lessons. One option is to have students read both endings and discuss both sets of discussion questions as a whole group. Another option is to have students choose an ending and focus on reading only that ending. Then they can discuss that ending's questions with a partner who made a similar choice before meeting together as a whole group to discuss both endings. Yet another option is to split the class into two sides and have each side read one ending and discuss that ending with their group. Then they can present and debate that side with the opposing choice.

Regardless of the chosen teaching strategy, the goal is to have students understand that there are different choices that the characters could make, and one choice in particular might be seen as the *wiser* choice of the two.

Of course, in real life there are often more than two options to consider when making a decision, and any decision can result in an infinite number of consequences. In this book only two options are provided, but you may want to encourage students to consider more possibilities and come up with their own third options. These third options can lead to discussions that are just as useful as those resulting from the provided options.

After students read the story and discuss the endings, they should make connections to their personal experiences. Give students the "What Would You Do?" written-response questions to answer independently. To conclude the unit, assign the "My Emotions" journal prompt, and give students the blank "My Emotions" template (page 71) to use. Additional journal templates (pages 72–76) are also included to expand on student's personal reflections. Bonus posters (pages 77–80) illustrate some of the coping strategies found in the units. They can be posted in the classroom or given to students for their personal use.

Dealing with Emotions

When teaching school-age children, it is important to first establish an awareness of emotions. Students might not have experience verbalizing their big feelings. Emotional literacy is simply giving students the vocabulary they need to talk about their feelings. You might want to start by showing students the *Emotions Chart* every day and asking them to point to the emotion they are feeling. You can expand on the emotions by sharing with students, "I feel happy today. What are some other words to describe how I am feeling?" (*joyful, excited, energetic, glad, cheerful, delighted*) Or, "I found a spider in my car this morning. Eeek! I was feeling afraid. What are some other words to describe how I was feeling?" (*frightened, scared, terrified, panicked*) Encourage students to explore different emotional vocabulary. Remind students that emotions are natural. Everyone is feeling an emotion at any time and sometimes we are feeling many emotions all at the same time!

So why do we need emotions? To start, emotions are what make us human! They are how we connect to ourselves, our friends, and our families. And long ago, emotions kept us alive. If a mountain lion or a snake were about to strike, we would need to fight back or run away. The limbic system in our brain would signal chemical reactions to happen in our body to make us react. Young students might not be aware of the connection between emotions and the physical body. The brain controls the emotions. Chemicals in the brain help us react to the danger. These chemicals also cause physical changes to happen.

Ask students what happens to their bodies when they are scared. (*Their hair might stand up, their heart beats faster, their muscles tense, but their bladder relaxes and their stomach slows down digestion.*) What happens when they are angry? (*Their heart beats faster, they breathe faster, they tense so much that their body feels hot and their face might turn red, they might even sweat or start to cry.*) What does their body feel like when they are sad? (*They scrunch up their face into a frown, their eyes water and cry tears, they feel tired and have less energy, their voice may even sound different.*) How does their body feel when they are happy? (*They smile, their body feels energized, they might laugh, their body might feel a warm glow.*)

Dealing with Emotions *(cont.)*

Talking about our emotions is not always an easy task. Most adults still struggle with this. Begin by reminding students that your classroom is a safe space to share their feelings. It is important that students know how to be good listeners and good friends. Encourage students to be helpful, kind, friendly, and encouraging to their peers at all times, but especially when someone is struggling with a big emotion.

How can you make your classroom feel like a safe and inviting place?

- Your classroom should be inviting, organized, and peaceful. Students need to see their work displayed throughout the room. This will not only give students a sense of belonging and ownership, it will teach them to celebrate their successes.

- If possible, create a mindfulness corner where students can relax if they are feeling stressed. It can contain stress balls, worry stones, stuffed animals, calming jars, books, etc. This space is not to be used as a punishment. Students will choose to visit it when they are feeling like they need a place of peace to calm down. Support students when they choose to visit the space and even take time to visit it yourself!

- Be present with students as they express their emotions. Give them the opportunity to identify how they are feeling. This can be done with a simple daily greeting and a "how are you feeling today?" Model your own emotional wellness by discussing how you are feeling as well. It is important for students to know that even their teacher has a bad day sometimes!

- Encourage students to trust and rely on one another. Project-based learning as a team is a great start. Make sure all students are engaged and mix up the groups. Use ice breakers, trust exercises, collaboration, and games.

- Use techniques to ensure that all students feel heard and included. Silent conversations are a great technique for less-verbal students. Instead of having a verbal group discussion, give groups a large sheet of chart paper and different-colored pens. Have them answer a main question and branch off and make comments and respond to one another, all through writing and drawing.

Emotions Chart

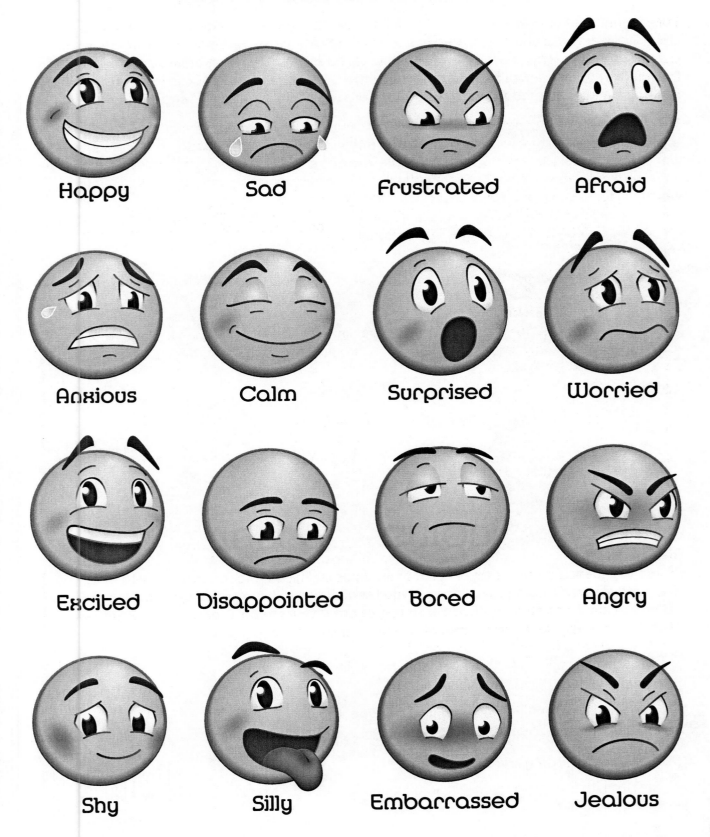

Happy

Sad

Frustrated

Afraid

Anxious

Calm

Surprised

Worried

Excited

Disappointed

Bored

Angry

Shy

Silly

Embarrassed

Jealous

Strategies

Coping strategies or skills are methods of helping us manage our emotions. While emotions are always valid and acceptable, it is ideal to learn skills to ease those big emotions before they become out of control. For example, it is okay for a child to feel angry if someone breaks their favorite toy. It is not okay to hit them or break something of theirs in return. If students can learn these healthy coping strategies at a young age, they will be more successful at managing stress as adults.

There are a variety of coping strategies that you can teach your students. Every child is unique and therefore some skills that work for one student may not work for another. Also, some coping strategies work better for certain emotions. For example, relaxing strategies work best to calm emotions like anger and frustration. Distracting strategies like telling jokes and spending time with your friends work best for sadness or anxiety. Expressive strategies like journaling help with anxiety and worry. Active strategies can be helpful to rebalance your energy due to any big emotion. Show students the *Strategies Chart* and encourage them to try all the skills.

Active Strategies

These strategies get your body moving! Active coping strategies work for all the emotions. When you are experiencing a big emotion, your brain sends chemicals through your body to make you aware and alert. These strategies can help you burn off that extra energy. Similarly, when you are feeling sad, tired, or bored, these active strategies can stimulate you. Exercise releases the good chemicals from your brain and signals you to feel happy.

Active strategies to teach your students:

- Yoga, stretching, balancing activities
- Jumping jacks, running, walking, jumping rope
- Team sports like baseball, basketball, soccer, or volleyball
- Gymnastics, dancing, martial arts, karate
- Small physical movements like tearing paper, squeezing a stress ball, or playing with a fidget spinner

Strategies *(cont.)*

Relaxing Strategies

These strategies help the body relax. Breathing exercises are helpful for all big emotions. Finding physical calm and mental peace can help ease the big emotions like anger and frustration.

Relaxing strategies to teach your students:

- Doing controlled breathing exercises like belly breathing
- Counting to ten slowly
- Taking a bath
- Drinking a cool glass of water or a warm cup of cocoa
- Making a fist, then relaxing it
- Petting an animal
- Practicing mindfulness (going on a walk, eating a snack, thinking about the five senses, etc.)

Distracting Strategies

These strategies help stop the cycle when thoughts about emotions make students feel worse. These strategies are especially helpful when feeling sad or anxious.

Distracting strategies to teach your students:

- Telling or listening to jokes
- Singing a favorite song
- Listening to music
- Spending time with family and friends
- Playing games with a pet
- Solving a puzzle
- Playing a board game or video game
- Learning to cook or bake something new

Expressive Strategies

These strategies help students think about and process their feelings. These skills are especially helpful for sadness, anxiety, and worry.

Expressive strategies to teach your students:

- Journaling about feelings
- Drawing or painting pictures that show the emotion
- Writing a song
- Talking about feelings with a friend or family member

Note: For additional strategies, see *Coping Skills for Kids Workbook* by Janine Halloran, M.A., LMHC. PESI Publishing & Media, PO Box 1000, Eau Claire, WI 54702-1000.

Strategies Chart

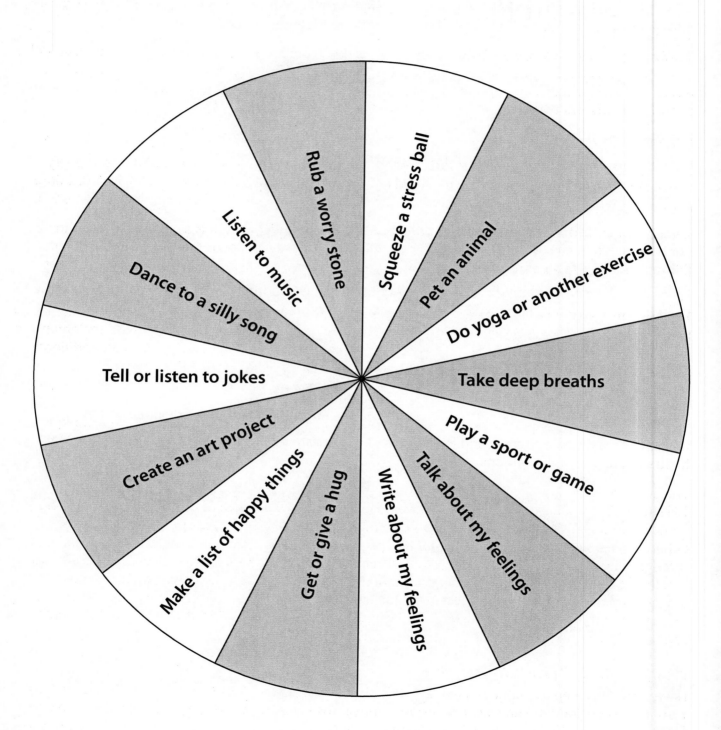

Understanding the Emotion: Anger

Summary

In this unit, students will read a story about a girl named London, who wants to play basketball at recess, but can't because the boys refuse to let girls play. London struggles to control her anger and has to make a choice: reacting physically or taking a moment to breathe and calm herself before choosing a different response.

Class Discussion

Spend a few minutes discussing the social-emotional vocabulary for this unit. Write the word *angry* on the board. Ask students to define the word for you, then write their responses on the board. If time permits, have students share their prior knowledge and experience with the class regarding this emotion.

Remind students that anger is a real emotion and it is okay to feel angry. It is a natural response in our bodies to a frustrating or stressful situation. Often our initial reaction is to want to lash out, but this may not be the best choice. Explain that there are skills we can learn to help us calm our bodies when we feel angry. When we are feeling calm, we tend to make better choices.

Tell students that they will be reading a story about a child who feels angry and has to make a choice. Read the story (pages 12–13) aloud or distribute copies of the story to students to read on their own. Have students choose an ending (page 14) either as a group or individually. (See page 4 for additional ideas for working with the stories and endings.)

Coping Skill Activity

Visual breathing techniques are a great tool for students to learn. Once they master these techniques, they can carry them as accessible tools to use throughout their lives when they find themselves in frustrating or stressful situations.

The goal of a breathing exercise is to get the body to relax when it is feeling an intense emotion. Tell students to visualize a flower. If you have access to real flowers, such as dandelions, provide one for each student. If they are using real flowers, students can keep their eyes open as they breathe. Otherwise, tell students to close their eyes and pretend they are smelling a flower. They will breathe in through their nose for a count of three, then pause for a count of three. Then, they will exhale all their breath out through their mouths to the count of three as they blow on the flower, trying to move the flower petals with their exhale. Practice the breathing exercise a few times with students and ask them to raise their hands if they feel more relaxed after the activity. Remind students that this exercise can be done at anytime, anywhere. They just need to breathe!

Personal Application

Have students come together as a whole group or in small groups to answer the discussion questions verbally. To conclude the unit, assign the written-response questions and the journal prompt as a way for students to relate the story to their own understanding of anger and how they have dealt with this emotion in their lives.

Basketball For All

"Nice shot!" London's dad exclaimed as the basketball swished through the hoop.

London grinned and chased the basketball before it rolled down the driveway. She loved playing basketball with her dad. It was always just the two of them for as long as she could remember. Every weeknight after work, London's dad would pick her up from her grandma's house. They would scarf down their dinner in order to shoot a few hoops in the driveway before the sun set. Initially, London would lose every single game. She would get frustrated and angry and sometimes she would scream and cry. Her dad would sit patiently and tell her to take deep breaths. Once London felt calm again, her dad would remind her that winning isn't everything. The game itself is where the fun is.

London's dad never played easy just because she was a child and instead played to the best of his ability and effortlessly won every game. But now that London was 11 years old, she was starting to be a competitive force against her dad.

"Not again!" London's dad laughed as his shot bounced off the rim. "You are way better than me!" he chuckled. "When did that happen? I feel like it was just yesterday that you learned to dribble the ball and could barely lift it over your head."

"Well, I have had years of practice. We've been playing almost every night since I was born," London said as she squinted her eyes with concentration. She gave a little hop as she threw the basketball as hard as she could. The ball sailed cleanly through the hoop. "Final point! My win!" London yelled as she collapsed on the driveway, exhausted from playing so hard.

"Excellent game," her dad said proudly. "You play like a professional! I am so amazed at how quickly your skills have improved." London stood up and gave her dad a tight hug and felt her cheeks ache from smiling so big. She scampered into the house as the last golden rays of sunshine disappeared behind the mountains.

The next day at school, London saw her best friend Sophie getting off the school bus. London beamed and ran over to greet her. Sophie and London had been friends since the first day of kindergarten when they met in line at school for breakfast. They both chose pancakes and juice and giggled after they simultaneously whispered "Yuck" when offered a tiny carton of white milk. Their mutual disgust of milk cemented their friendship and the two girls were inseparable ever since that day. Sophie smiled as soon as she saw London approaching.

"I beat my dad again last night in basketball," London said excitedly.

"No way! That's fantastic! Let's play basketball today at recess," answered Sophie.

"Deal!" declared London as the girls headed over to line up for class.

When their fifth-grade class was dismissed for recess, the girls grabbed a basketball from the sports bin and skipped over to the basketball courts. A group of boys were already on the main court and were dividing themselves up into two teams. "Should we ask to play too?" London asked Sophie.

But Sophie's face turned red as she looked down at her feet and mumbled, "No way. Colson is playing basketball. He is a mean bully and he never lets girls play, so let's just go do something else."

Basketball for All (cont.)

London stared at the boys on the court and shouted, "Hey, can we play?"

Colson strutted over and laughed in her face. "Girls don't play basketball. You're just not as good as we are. You could bring us some water to drink, though," he added with a smirk.

London felt her fists clench and her face flush red and hot. Her heart was beating quickly in her chest and all she could think about was slapping the smirk off of Colson's face. But Sophie grabbed her arm and pulled her away. "He's not worth getting into trouble over, so let's just go."

London sighed and walked away, but she could feel the rage inside her still bubbling. She turned and glared at Colson, but he was already involved in the basketball game.

That night after dinner, London's dad grabbed the basketball and grinned. "I'm ready to get whomped again by your superb skills!"

But London just frowned and grumbled, "Dad, do you think girls can play basketball as well as boys can?"

London's dad looked concerned and answered, "Of course. You beat me last night, remember? Where is this coming from?"

London wanted to tell her dad about Colson, but she didn't want to make it into a big deal. "I was just thinking about it. Never mind, let's go play!" she yelled as she snatched the basketball out of her dad's hand and bounded out onto the driveway.

The following day at recess, London was determined to play basketball. Sophie left school early for a dentist appointment, so London was ready to confront Colson on her own. She marched over to the basketball courts with clenched fists and unwavering bravery as Colson was dividing the boys on the court into teams. London ran up to him and firmly demanded, "Hey, I am playing basketball today. Whose team am I on?"

Colson sneered at London and hissed, "I told you yesterday that girls aren't playing basketball with us."

London glared back and said, "I am just as good as you are, and I have every right to play."

Colson laughed and said, "Oh yeah? Catch!" He chucked the basketball as hard as he could, and it caught London off guard. The ball slammed into her stomach and slightly knocked the wind out of her. She gasped for breath and felt the anger intensifying and expanding inside of her. Her fists were clenched so tightly that she felt her nails piercing into the skin of her palms. London glared at Colson and took a few steps toward him as the anger took control of her body and clouded her thoughts. Colson was a bully and she wanted him to pay for his actions.

Should London hit Colson?

Making Choices

Choice 1—Yes

London allowed the anger to rise up and take control. She picked up the basketball and threw it with all of her might directly at Colson's face. Colson screamed as the ball slammed into his nose just before London shoved him hard and he stumbled back onto the blacktop. Blood poured from his nose as he cupped his hands around his face. The other students stared silently at London. "I think you broke my nose," Colson mumbled as tears streamed down his face.

The playground supervisor blew her whistle and ran over to assist Colson. She looked at London sternly and told her to head to the principal's office. London nodded and slowly walked towards the office. Her heart was pounding in her chest and her brow was furrowed. She thought attacking Colson would make her feel better, but instead she just felt worse.

At that moment, Colson's best friend Seth caught up to her and softly said, "The other guys and I would have let you play. Next time for sure, okay?" London nodded her head in agreement, but she felt remorse and embarrassment for what she did. She felt the dread in her stomach as she entered the principal's office.

London explained what happened on the basketball court as Principal Thomas silently took notes. He looked at London with concern and told her that while Colson was out of line and had no authority to tell the girls they can't play, she broke school rules with her violent outburst and would be suspended for the rest of the week. London's heart sank. "Next time, use your voice. Take a stand and tell someone. We can help you solve the problem without violence," Principal Thomas said calmly. London nodded quietly and wished she had tried to calm her anger before reacting against Colson.

Choice 2—No

London slowly took a deep breath, closed her eyes for a moment, and tried to calm the boiling rage inside of her. As she exhaled, she felt her fists relax. She calmly retrieved the basketball and started to dribble it. Then she looked over at Colson's friend Seth and confidently proclaimed, "Colson doesn't think girls can play but I disagree. What do you think?"

Seth smiled at London and said, "I think you're probably better than most of us. I see you playing basketball with your dad all the time. You can definitely play."

The other boys stood behind Seth and nodded in agreement as Colson shrugged with irritation. "Fine," he murmured. "But she's on your team, Seth."

London passed the ball to Colson and jogged onto the court. She felt a smile start to spread across her face as she realized that she had handled the situation and managed her anger. London played as hard as she could and right before the bell rang, she passed the ball to Seth, who scored the final point to win. He ran over and high-fived her with a big grin. "You can play on our team anytime," he exclaimed.

Colson mumbled, "Good game," to London as he walked off the court. London beamed. She was proud of herself for standing up to Colson, and she knew she was just as good as the boys.

What Do You Think?

Choice 1

1. Why do you think London attacked Colson? Do you think she felt better or worse after she did this?

2. Do you think Colson deserved to be hurt?

3. Do you think London agreed with the principal's decision to suspend her? Why or why not?

4. What did London learn about her anger?

Choice 2

1. What did London do that helped control her anger?

2. Do you think Colson will let London play again the next time?

3. Do you think London felt as though she handled the situation well?

4. How do you think Colson felt when London stood up for herself? Do you think he learned a lesson?

What Would You Do?

1 Have you ever been excluded from a game, event, or group? How did you feel?

_____

_____

_____

_____

_____

2 Have you ever pushed someone? How did you feel after?

_____

_____

_____

_____

_____

3 List one or more things you can do to calm down when you are feeling angry.

_____

_____

_____

_____

_____

My Emotions: Anger

Think about London's story. Have you ever been angry with someone at school? Were they acting like a bully? How did you handle your anger then? How would you handle your anger now? Write about your experience and what you have learned.

Understanding the Emotion: Happiness

Summary

In this unit, students will read a story about Aiden, a sixth grader who learns that it's important to find happiness in helping others, instead of only focusing on himself.

Class Discussion

Spend a few minutes discussing the social-emotional vocabulary for this unit. Write the word *happy* on the board. Ask students to define the word for you, then write their responses on the board. If time permits, have students share their prior knowledge and experience with the class regarding this emotion.

Remind students that feeling happy is a good emotion. When we are happy, our bodies feel different. Sometimes, we feel energized. Happiness is described as a warm, fuzzy feeling inside. Studies show that happiness is an emotion that helps us in many ways. When we are happy, we are healthier. We get along better with our friends and family. And, happiness can be contagious! If we are happy and full of laughter, we can help spread that happiness to others who may not be feeling so happy.

Tell students that they will be reading a story about a boy who finds happiness playing video games with his friends. However, after an earthquake destroys a town, his grandma urges him to take action to help. He has to decide whether to participate in a video game tournament with his friends or assist his grandma at a fundraiser. Read the story (pages 18–19) aloud or distribute copies of the story to students to read on their own. Have students choose an ending (page 20) either as a group or individually. (See page 4 for additional ideas for working with the stories and endings.)

Coping Skill Activity

Happiness is an emotion we strive to feel. There are ways to find happiness if we are feeling sad or just feeling blah. Exercise can make us happy. Spending time with our favorite people can make us happy. Laughter can brighten our days. One important skill to learn is that helping others find their happiness can also increase our own. You can visually explain this to students with a popular balloon activity. Blow up one balloon for each student in the class and have them write their name on it. You can do this ahead of time if needed. Randomly scatter the balloons throughout your classroom. Tell students you are going to give them one minute to try to find their own balloon, which represents their happiness. Set the timer and go! Most likely, very few students will be able to find their own balloon and things may feel a bit chaotic. Gather the class together and try again, only this time, tell students to grab one balloon and hand it to the student it belongs to. Explain that when we help others find their happiness, things are peaceful and we in turn find our own happiness.

Personal Application

Have students come together as a whole group or in small groups to answer the discussion questions verbally. To conclude the unit, assign the written-response questions and the journal prompt as a way for students to relate the story to their own understanding of happiness and times they have felt this emotion in their lives.

Donating Happiness

"We destroyed the dragon!" Aiden cried happily into his headset. He was playing his favorite online video game with his best friend, Jake.

"That was the best victory ever!" Jake's voice came through Aiden's headset and it made him grin. He loved spending time with his best friend, and it was great that they could stay connected to each other online even when they weren't hanging out in person. Every Saturday morning, they both woke up early to play video games together while still in their pajamas. They loved creating new worlds and finding creative new ways to beat the levels. Aiden and Jake could talk to each other through their headsets about every little thing, including what they were each eating for breakfast. It was the highlight of Aiden's week. Aiden lived with his grandma, who tried to get him to do other things on the weekend, but he often refused. Video gaming was his passion, and it made him feel happy and energized.

"Aiden, turn off the video game, please. We need to watch the news," his grandmother said anxiously as she briskly walked into the room. "There was an earthquake this morning where your uncle George lives. I am worried about him. I have tried calling, but I haven't been able to reach him."

Aiden said goodbye to Jake and turned off the video game console. "I am sure it will be okay, Grandma," Aiden said, but he could hear the worry in his own voice.

The newscaster was talking about the homes that were ruined by the earthquake and showed hundreds of people gathering at disaster relief centers because they had nowhere else to go. Tears were streaming down Aiden's grandmother's cheeks. Aiden gave his grandmother a big hug. "Grandma, let me use your phone to text Uncle George. I read somewhere once that text messages might go through more easily than phone calls," Aiden declared. He located his uncle George's number on his grandmother's cell phone and typed a short text that read, "Are you okay?"

Immediately, his uncle George texted back, "Yes. We are all fine. I am helping my neighbors clean up some broken glass." Aiden read the text aloud to his grandmother and her eyes brightened. She wiped the tears away from her face.

Aiden put his arm around his grandmother's shoulder. "Is there something we can do to help?" he asked.

His grandmother took a deep breath and smiled. "Let's find out!" she said with a determined look on her face. She took her phone from Aiden and made a quick phone call. She hung up the phone and turned back to Aiden. "Today, we can help sort cans of food at the food bank," she said. "Get dressed and come with me."

Aiden nodded. He wanted to finish playing his video game with Jake, but he knew he had to listen to his grandmother. He quickly got dressed and brushed his teeth. They walked out of their apartment building together and headed through the crowded city street to the bus stop.

Donating Happiness *(cont.)*

The food bank was bustling with volunteers all eager to help in some way. Aiden and his grandmother were given the task of checking expiration dates on cans and then loading them into crates. Aiden wrote the number of cans on the crate and then stacked the heavy crates on top of one another in the corner. It was tedious work, and he was tired and sweaty at the end of the day. On the walk back to the bus station, his grandma suggested they stop for a treat. They each had a tall, refreshing glass of lemonade and shared a giant salted soft pretzel. Aiden's grandmother smiled at him and said, "Thank you for joining me. I feel better already. I like to feel helpful and volunteering at the food bank makes me feel happy. Next week, we can volunteer at a fundraiser to raise money for the earthquake disaster relief group."

Aiden paused and realized that he felt happy too. He was grinning, and his body felt energized after drinking the cold lemonade. He enjoyed spending the day with his grandma and seeing her happy made him feel happy too. He also felt useful, and his good deed for the day made him feel as though he was making a difference in the world. Aiden and his grandmother smiled at each other as they walked the rest of the way to the bus stop.

The next Saturday morning, Aiden woke up early. He poured himself a bowl of his favorite cereal, placed his headset on his head, and turned on his video game console. Jake's sleepy voice came through the headset with a groggy, "Hi Aiden. I just woke up. I am so excited to play today. There's a tournament today that we can play in together! Let's try to defeat the final boss."

Aiden grinned and said, "We can totally do it! I have been thinking up new strategies all week!"

Just as they were starting their first game, Aiden's grandma walked into the room. "Aiden, today is the fundraiser, remember? You said you would come with me. I signed up to work at the ticket counter, and you can help the volunteers wash cars. Your favorite taco stand will be there too! I'll buy us lunch afterwards," she said with a grin.

Aiden groaned. He did not want to go wash cars at the fundraiser. He just wanted to play in the video game tournament with Jake. Aiden looked at his grandma's eager smile and his heart sank. He knew it would make her so happy if he came with her to the fundraiser.

Should Aiden help his grandmother at the fundraiser?

Making Choices

Choice 1–Yes

Aiden wanted to help his grandmother because he knew it would make her happy. Plus, he really did enjoy volunteering at the food bank and remembered how it made him feel happy too. Aiden quickly told Jake that he had to go but would be able to play video games later that night.

Jake said it was okay and that he understood. Aiden rushed to get dressed and he walked with his grandma down the street to the community center parking lot. He signed up to help wash the cars and joined a group of students from his school who were also helping. They had a blast as they laughed and told jokes while scrubbing the cars clean. The sun was shining, and the day was beautiful.

Aiden looked over at his grandma selling tickets at the booth and saw that she was smiling too. He realized that doing things for other people could bring him the same buzzing and energized feeling of happiness that he got when he played his video games.

After the last car was washed, Aiden's grandma walked over with a plate of his favorite tacos. Aiden gave his grandma a hug as he said, "Thank you, Grandma. Today was a really fantastic day." His grandma's face beamed with happiness.

Choice 2–No

Aiden didn't want to wash the cars for the fundraiser and would rather play in the video game tournament with Jake. He looked at his grandma and mumbled, "Grandma, I don't feel well, and I don't think I will be able to go."

His grandma looked concerned and placed her hand across his forehead. "You don't feel warm," she said. "I will stay home to take care of you."

Aiden suddenly felt his heart hurt in his chest. He didn't want his grandma to miss out on the fundraiser, but what could he say now? "You need to get back in bed if you are unwell," his grandma said. "I will make you soup for lunch."

Aiden sighed and ambled slowly back to his bedroom. He remained in bed for an hour staring at the ceiling and pondering his decision when he heard a knock on his door.

His grandma asked if he needed anything. Aiden sat up in bed and regretfully confessed, "I feel fine, Grandma. I wanted to stay home and play video games and I am sorry for not telling the truth. Do you think there is still time for us to go volunteer?"

His grandma looked disappointed. "I assumed you wanted to volunteer with me," she said.

"I promise I do. I was only thinking about myself and not wanting to miss my video game tournament. But I can always play video games, and this fundraiser is important," Aiden answered.

His grandma's face softened as she said, "Thank you for telling me. There is still time today if you want to go. Plus, tacos are much more delicious than soup for lunch."

Aiden grinned. "Thank you, Grandma," he said and jumped out of bed to get ready.

What Do You Think?

Choice 1

1. Why did Aiden choose to go to the fundraiser?

2. How do you think Aiden's grandma felt?

3. What did Aiden learn about happiness?

4. Do you think Aiden will volunteer more with his grandma?

Choice 2

1. Why did Aiden's heart hurt when his grandma said she would stay home to take care of him?

2. How do you think Aiden felt when he was lying in his bed alone?

3. What did Aiden learn about happiness?

4. Do you think Aiden will have fun at the fundraiser?

What Would You Do?

1 Have you ever done something to make someone else happy? How did it make you feel?

_____

_____

_____

_____

_____

2 Have you ever volunteered for a good cause? How did it make you feel?

_____

_____

_____

_____

_____

_____

3 List five things that make you happy.

_____

_____

_____

_____

_____

My Emotions: Happiness

Think about Aiden and how he learned that helping others can bring him happiness. Write about your experience sharing happiness and what you have learned.

Understanding the Emotion:
Sadness

Summary

In this unit, students will read a story about Brian and Autumn, a brother and sister who have to move to a new neighborhood because of their parents' divorce. They are feeling sad and lonely and miss their old home and friends. When Autumn decides to meet new kids in the neighborhood to shake off her sadness, Brian has to choose whether to join her or stay home.

Class Discussion

Spend a few minutes discussing the social-emotional vocabulary for this unit. Write the word *sad* on the board. Ask students to define the word for you, then write their responses on the board. If time permits, have students share their prior knowledge and experience with the class regarding this emotion.

Tell students that everyone feels sadness at times. It can be due to a situation such as a pet dying, a loved one moving away, or your team losing a game. Other times, we may feel sadness for no specific reason. We all get the blues from time to time. A helpful way to manage sadness is to know that just like any other emotion, it will pass. It may take a few minutes or a few days, but sadness will not last forever. When we are sad, our bodies feel different. We might feel our heart ache or we might cry. Sadness can make us tired or even change our appetites. As with every emotion, there are things you can do to help manage sadness. Talking about sadness is helpful because it releases some of the emotion. Also, doing things that we enjoy can make us feel less sad. Lastly, exercise is another great way to help with sadness. If our bodies are moving, it helps to distract us from the sad feelings and it can build our energy and joy.

Tell students that they will be reading a story about two children who are sad when their parents divorce and they have to move. They are faced with different choices as they manage their sadness. Read the story (pages 24–25) aloud or distribute copies of the story to students to read on their own. Have students choose an ending (page 26) either as a group or individually. (See page 4 for additional ideas for working with the stories and endings.)

Coping Skill Activity

Exercise can help with many emotions, and sadness is one of them! Often when we feel sad, we search for ways to cheer ourselves up. This coping skill combines laughter, joy, and exercise all in one: lead a silly dance party! Find a list of silly songs that you can play for students. (Parry Gripp is a musician whose songs will get your students moving and giggling.) Tell students that they need to move their bodies in silly, goofy ways for the duration of the song. The goal is to keep moving continuously until the song ends. After the laughter and dancing ends, ask students how they are feeling. Did the silly dancing make them smile? Giggle? Did the exercise give them energy?

Personal Application

Have students come together as a whole group or in small groups to answer the discussion questions verbally. To conclude the unit, assign the written-response questions and the journal prompt as a way for students to relate the story to their own understanding of feeling sad and how they have dealt with this emotion in their lives.

Homesick

"I hate this," Brian said glumly as he threw another book into a box. "I don't want to move, and I don't want to pack up my stuff, and I don't want to live in the boring country. There's going to be nothing to do," he whined as he gazed out his bedroom window, which overlooked the busy lights of the city below. "I want to stay in the city with all our friends. Why are they making us move?" he complained to his sister, Autumn.

"Because Mom and Dad are getting divorced, and Mom got a new job in the country," Autumn said sadly as she packed her favorite stuffed koala and blanket into a box. "This whole thing is so sad, and I don't know how we are ever going to feel happy again," she whispered as a tear ran down her face. She collapsed on her bare mattress and stared up at the twinkling lights that dangled from the canopy above her bed.

Brian sat down on his bed across the room and put his head in his hands. "I feel tired and sad all the time. I have no energy and just want to stay in bed," he groaned. "Plus, I hate seeing Mom and Dad so sad. I don't understand why they couldn't just solve their problems. Everything is changing and it's horrible."

Autumn closed her eyes and sighed deeply. They had been sharing their big room in the high-rise apartment in the city since they were babies. All her memories were of this apartment and this room. She fell asleep every night to the hum of traffic noise and, on the warm summer nights that they slept with the windows open, the sugary smell of waffle cones from the ice cream shop below. Autumn snuggled against her pillow, which was the only thing left that she hadn't packed. Her heart had felt so heavy for weeks since she found out about her parents' divorce. She took one more deep breath and opened her eyes.

"Brian, I know the sadness is overwhelming, but let's be positive and list all the good things. We finally get our own rooms. We have that huge cornfield behind the new house to run through, and we have enough grass in the backyard to play soccer. Dad's new apartment is still in the city, so we can visit all our old friends when we stay with him." Autumn instantly felt a little of the weight lift off her chest and a twinge of excitement for the new changes.

Brian lifted his head and looked straight at Autumn. "There is nothing positive about what's going on. Not one single thing. I hate all of it, and I just want my life back," he said sadly as he packed his last box of books. He took one last look at his room, and then turned around and walked out for the last time.

Autumn and Brian spent the entire weekend moving into the new house in the country. Even though it was just an hour away from the city, it felt like a completely different world. Their high-rise apartment building full of people was replaced with a cozy cream-colored house with faded green trim and gray shutters. It was tucked behind a row of big trees and overlooked a nearby farm's cornfield. The crumbling sidewalks wound around the neighborhood and everything seemed so quiet and spaced apart.

Homesick (cont.)

Autumn felt a sense of relief as their car turned onto their street and she saw a group of neighborhood kids riding bikes together up and down the meandering sidewalk. "Proof of life," she giggled as she poked Brian in the ribs in an attempt to get him to smile. But he just sighed and stared out the car window.

"It's beautiful," Autumn whispered to her mom as they ate dinner on the back porch and watched the sun set behind the rows of corn.

"I feel like we stepped back in time, but not in a good way," Brian huffed sarcastically.

Their mom smiled. "I know this is a big change for all of us, but this will feel like home to you someday. Just give it some time," she said. Autumn smiled back at her mom. The sadness of the divorce and the move still ached in her heart, but she was determined to embrace her new life with as much optimism as possible. She wanted to feel happy again. She glanced over at Brian who was still sulking behind his untouched plate of dinner.

Suddenly, Autumn had an idea. She ran into the house and turned on Brian's favorite dance song so loudly that they could hear it on the back porch.

Autumn's mom grinned. "Dance party?" she asked.

"Oh yes," Autumn giggled, and she began to jump around and twirl with her mom as they practiced their silliest dance moves. She saw Brian smile slightly for one moment, even though he refused to join in the dance. When the song ended, Autumn fell back into her chair and said breathlessly, "Well, at least I feel better." Brian rolled his eyes in return and stared silently at the setting sun.

The next morning, Autumn sat on the front porch and wrote in her journal. She always felt better after writing down her feelings and experiences. She decided that today she would ride her bike around the neighborhood in hopes of meeting the other kids.

Brian walked out onto the porch and asked Autumn what she was doing. "Finding happiness," Autumn declared. She grabbed Brian's arm and dragged him over to the garage. "Today, we are going to ride our bikes and make some new friends," Autumn said with a nervous but determined tone.

Brian groaned. "No way," he mumbled. "I don't need new friends. I am happy with my friends back home."

Autumn looked at Brian and softly said, "But this is our home, and we have to try to make it a happy one. The exercise will help you feel better." But Brian felt the burden of sadness weighing down his shoulders. He could not imagine finding his happiness here. He knew what made him happy, and this new place was not it. He just wanted to go back to his old home.

Should Brian join Autumn on the bike ride?

Making Choices

Choice 1—Yes

Brian saw the hopeful look on his sister's face, so he nodded and retrieved his bike. He really didn't feel like riding his bike, but he wanted Autumn to be happy. He trailed after Autumn down the crumbling, dilapidated sidewalk. He wondered about the history of the neighborhood and thought it might be interesting to do some research.

As Autumn pumped her legs faster, Brian grinned and tried to catch up to her. The cool morning breeze felt refreshing on his skin, and the air smelled like pine trees and grass. He inhaled deeply and began to feel aware of his senses again. Everything had felt numb and dull when he was focused on his sadness, but as he pedaled faster and felt the freedom of coasting along on his bike, his body felt lighter, as though he were shedding the weight of sadness with every rotation of his legs. He caught up to Autumn and teased, "Still faster than you, sister."

Suddenly, a group of kids approached on their bikes. "Hey, are you the new family at the end of the street?" a boy called out curiously. Autumn nodded. "Do you guys like to play soccer?" he asked. "We're headed to the field to play, and we could always use new players."

Autumn turned and waited for Brian's response. He grinned. "Yeah, we'd love to play soccer."

Autumn did a little happy dance as she turned her bike around to follow the kids to the field. "See, it already feels better, right?" she asked Brian. He beamed in return and realized it was the first time in months that he didn't feel sad.

Choice 2—No

Brian felt crushingly sad, and the thought of riding his bike around this neighborhood was not how he envisioned his day. He didn't want to accept the new house and the new neighborhood and his parents' divorce. He wanted to pretend it wasn't happening. He scowled at Autumn, shook his head no, and headed back to sit on the front porch alone.

"Well, I am going without you!" Autumn cried as she pushed off on her bike and pedaled down the street.

Just then, the door swung open and Brian's mom came outside. She sat down next to him on the porch. "I know you are sad and it feels overwhelming, and those feelings are normal. But moping around the house isn't going to help those feelings go away. You need to explore and get exercise and meet new people. You might actually find that you enjoy it here," she said softly, then she stood up and retreated to the house.

Brian knew his mom was right, but he didn't know where to begin. He sat on the porch for an hour and tried to think of the positive things. He did love having his own room where he could listen to his music, and he even got to paint the walls his favorite shade of blue. Thinking about the positives made Brian feel a little better. Suddenly, he heard Autumn shouting his name in the distance as she pedaled excitedly up the driveway.

"Brian, I met a bunch of new friends! We played soccer but after a few rounds I came home to get some water. We need an extra player," Autumn said breathlessly. Brian smiled and agreed to come along before walking over to the garage to find his bike.

What Do You Think?

Choice 1

1. Why did Brian choose to join his sister on the bike ride?

2. How did Brian feel when he was riding his bike?

3. What are some things that helped Autumn feel less sad?

4. Do you think Brian will find happiness in his new home?

Choice 2

1. Why did Brian choose to stay home?

2. Do you think talking to his mom helped Brian?

3. How did focusing on positive thoughts ease the feeling of sadness?

4. Do you think Brian will have fun playing soccer?

What Would You Do?

1 Have you ever had to move to a new place? How did you feel?

_____

_____

_____

_____

_____

2 Do you think you would act more like Autumn or Brian if you were in that situation? Why?

_____

_____

_____

_____

_____

_____

3 List five things that help you feel better when you are sad.

_____

_____

_____

_____

_____

_____

My Emotions: Sadness

Think about Brian and Autumn's experience with their parents' divorce and moving to a new home. Have you ever gone through something similar, or do you know someone who has? Write about your experience with this kind of sadness and what you have learned.

Understanding the Emotion: Fear

Summary

In this unit, students will read a story about a girl named Quinn who is afraid of a mean girl at school named Regina. After feeling bullied by Regina for weeks, Quinn wants to take action and has to choose how she will confront Regina.

Class Discussion

Spend a few minutes discussing the social-emotional vocabulary for this unit. Write the word *afraid* on the board. Ask students to define the word for you, then write their responses on the board. If time permits, have students share their prior knowledge and experience with the class regarding this emotion. You might want to address the concept of bullying to make sure students have a clear understanding of what a bully does.

Remind students that fear is a natural feeling. We often feel afraid in order to protect ourselves. For example, if we see a poisonous snake, we will probably be afraid to touch it. That fear protects us from getting bit! When we feel afraid, our bodies tense and our hearts beat faster. Our hands might shake and our mouths may feel dry. When the threat or fear goes away, our body will start to relax again.

Tell students that they will be reading a story about a girl who has to choose how to deal with her fear of a bully at school. Read the story (pages 30–31) aloud or distribute copies of the story to students to read on their own. Have students choose an ending (page 32) either as a group or individually. (See page 4 for additional ideas for working with the stories and endings.)

Coping Skill Activity

When we feel afraid, our bodies react. It doesn't matter if we are scared of the dark, jumping into a pool, or standing up to a bully. The best way to calm our fear is to face the situation head-on. But when we feel afraid, that seems like the last thing we want to do! So, we can use special breathing skills to relax our bodies. This feeling of relaxation and peace will help us face our fears. It can clear our minds, and the thing we are afraid of won't feel quite so scary.

Teach students a breathing exercise called "belly breathing." Have students sit on the floor with their legs crossed. Have them gently rest their hands on their bellies. Tell students to close their eyes and inhale a big breath into their bellies. They want to inhale so much air that they feel their bellies expand like big balloons! Then, tell students to slowly exhale all the air out and feel their tummies shrink. Repeat this exercise a few times, and ask students how they feel after the belly breathing. (See page 79 for a bonus poster illustrating belly breathing.)

Personal Application

Have students come together as a whole group or in small groups to answer the discussion questions verbally. To conclude the unit, assign the written-response questions and the journal prompt as a way for students to relate the story to their own understanding of being afraid and times they have felt this emotion in their lives.

The Confrontation

"Here comes Quinn," taunted Regina loudly as the school cafeteria filled with sixth graders eager to eat lunch. "Good thing your parents gave you a boy's name since you never dress like a girl."

Quinn felt her face burn red with embarrassment as Regina continued her attacks. "Why do you dress like that? You know you're supposed to be a girl, right?" Regina sneered with disgust as she pointed at Quinn's basketball shoes, cargo shorts, baggy T-shirt, and short haircut.

Quinn whispered, "These clothes are comfortable for me," as she grabbed her lunch tray and hurried to sit next to her best friend, Ari, who was saving her a place at the lunch table. Quinn's hands were shaking as she set her tray down and slid onto the bench.

Ari noticed the familiar look of fear on her face and said gently, "Why do you let her talk to you like that? She is so mean to you and you just let her continue to be awful."

Quinn sighed and replied, "I never know what to say to Regina. I feel so afraid of her because I never know what she is going to do. Every time she teases me, I feel so small and want to hide."

Ari nodded with sympathy but said, "You really should talk to someone about her. She acts like a bully, and the school won't tolerate that."

Quinn just shrugged and answered, "I'm afraid to tell someone because if she gets in trouble the mean comments could just get worse."

Ari nodded in agreement. "You're probably right, but I still hate seeing her talk to you that way." Quinn smiled at her best friend's support and handed her a cookie from her lunch tray as a thank you.

Quinn ate her sandwich and gazed over at Regina sitting in the center of the cafeteria, eating her lunch and smiling as if she didn't have a care in the world. A few years ago, Quinn and Regina had been friends. But something shifted, and Regina began hanging out with new friends and seemed to want nothing to do with Quinn. She teased Quinn for not dressing the way the other girls did. There were a few times that Regina passed Quinn in the hallway and intentionally bumped Quinn so hard that Quinn stumbled. She didn't understand why Regina was so mean to her, but as the teasing increased, Quinn's fear of Regina did too.

A week ago, Regina posted a photo of Quinn from when they were friends in second grade to her social media account. She tagged Quinn in it, and the caption read, "Long ago, Quinn really was a girl." Quinn felt humiliated. Ari was always reminding her that she needed to tell someone about Regina's behavior, but the fear held Quinn back. She was afraid that everyone would somehow side with Regina. The other kids often laughed when Regina made comments about Quinn. Instead of reacting, Quinn chose to spend most of her time as far away from Regina as possible.

That afternoon, Quinn and Ari were walking home from school together just like they always did. They went their separate ways after reaching the tiny market in the center of town. They each lived in neighborhoods on the opposite sides of the main shopping center. Quinn loved the familiarity and safety of her small town. The girls waved goodbye as they parted, and Ari told Quinn she'd call her that night to work on their math homework.

The Confrontation (cont.)

Quinn smiled and felt the warm sun shining on her face. She stopped inside the market to buy herself a drink. The store manager greeted her warmly and asked how her school day had gone. Quinn shrugged and said, "It was okay, but I am glad it's over," as she handed him a dollar for her cup of lemonade. She turned and left the market and ran right into Regina and a group of three other girls.

Regina rolled her eyes when she saw Quinn. "Ugh. I thought I got rid of you at school, but you seem to just show up everywhere I go," Regina quipped.

Quinn tried not to make eye contact as she felt her palms grow sweaty and her heart rate increase. Regina was terrifying, and Quinn didn't know what to expect from her. Regina glared at Quinn and said, "Step aside," before giving Quinn a slight bump as she pushed past to walk into the market. Quinn lost her grip on the lemonade, and it spilled all over her shirt and the street. "Nice one," Regina laughed, and the other girls giggled and followed her into the market, leaving Quinn on the sidewalk dripping with lemonade. Quinn felt the tears welling in her eyes as she picked up her lemonade cup, threw it in the trash, and walked the rest of the way home.

When Quinn got home, she called Ari and told her what happened. Ari listened quietly and responded that she would support Quinn in whatever she needed to do but urged her to report the bullying. Quinn agreed and decided to talk to her dad.

During dinner, Quinn was so lost in thought wondering what she could do to face Regina that she barely touched her food. Her dad asked if she was okay, and she exhaled slowly and replied, "Dad, do you remember Regina? We used to be friends." Her dad nodded. "She's bullying me at school, and I'm afraid of her. She teases me and embarrasses me every day. I want to get back at her by doing something to show her what it feels like to be bullied."

Her dad frowned and gave her a hug. "You need to stand up to Regina and tell her to stop. If she doesn't stop, then we need to talk to your teacher. However, bullying her back is not the right choice, Quinn. Don't lower yourself to that level," her dad said gently.

The next morning as Quinn got ready for school, she felt clammy and shaky. She realized that she was afraid to face Regina, and she hadn't worked out a plan. Quinn thought about her conversation with her dad and knew he wanted her to confront Regina and tell her teacher about the bullying. But Quinn dreaded the confrontation. She remembered a photo she had of Regina from when they were friends in second grade. They had a crazy and silly hairstyle party. Quinn thought that if she posted the photo online, Regina would be mortified and maybe that would show her how it feels to be bullied.

Should Quinn post the photo of Regina?

Making Choices

Choice 1—Yes

Quinn didn't stop to think about the consequences of posting the photo. She wanted revenge against Regina and posting the photo was easier and less scary than confronting her face-to-face. She posted the photo on her social media account and tagged Regina and included the hashtag "#loser." Then she finished getting ready and walked to school.

As soon as she reached school, Ari walked up to her and said nervously, "Quinn, you shouldn't have posted that photo. I heard that Regina showed it to her mom, and now I'm worried that you'll get in trouble." Quinn felt the fear rise up in her chest, and she realized that she was going to look like the bully now. She didn't feel more powerful than Regina. She just felt bad about herself for doing the same thing Regina did to her.

As the school bell rang, everyone headed for class and Quinn felt a shove as Regina passed by and hissed in her ear, "You'll get what you deserve for that."

Quinn realized that trying to bully Regina wasn't going to fix her problem and that she should have listened to her dad and reported Regina first. After school, Quinn got called into the principal's office and was surprised to see her dad already waiting for her. She fought back the tears as she explained what she did. She tried to show them the photo that Regina had posted of her, but Regina had deleted it.

Quinn's face burned with embarrassment. Her dad explained the bullying situation to the principal but told Quinn that he was disappointed in her retaliation. The principal told Quinn to delete the photo and that she would meet with both her and Regina to work out the situation and determine the correct disciplinary action. Quinn nodded her head solemnly.

Choice 2—No

Quinn got ready for school and thought about the photo. Initially, she thought it might make her feel better to get revenge against Regina. But she knew that bullying is wrong, and she didn't want to act like Regina. Instead, she decided it was time to confront her fear and face Regina.

At school, Quinn asked Ari if she would be her support. Ari agreed and together they marched determinedly up to Regina, who was surrounded by her group of friends. Quinn felt her palms grow sweaty and shaky, and she felt a chill on her arms. She paused for a moment and closed her eyes and tried to calm the fear. "What do you want?" Regina jeered.

Quinn looked Regina straight in the eyes and said, "You need to stop bullying me now or else I will report it. Delete the mean photo you posted of me. Do not touch me or talk to me again."

Regina shrugged her shoulders, rolled her eyes, and declared, "You're not worth my time anyway," before turning and walking away.

Quinn exhaled slowly and Ari's face broke into a huge grin. "You did it," Ari whispered. Quinn felt her body shaking as she calmed down with a few more deep breaths. She knew she would never be friends with Regina but believed that the bullying would stop. That night, she told her dad what she said to Regina. He proclaimed that he was so proud of her for confronting her fear and reminded her that if Regina tried anything again, Quinn needed to involve her teacher. Quinn promised that she would.

What Do You Think?

Choice 1

1. Why did Quinn post the photo of Regina?

2. How do you think Regina felt when she saw the photo?

3. Do you think Quinn regretted her decision?

4. What do you think will happen when Regina and Quinn meet with the principal?

Choice 2

1. Why did Quinn decide not to post the photo?

2. Do you think having Ari with her gave Quinn more confidence?

3. How did Quinn calm her fear enough to approach Regina?

4. Do you think Regina will try to bully Quinn in the future?

What Would You Do?

1 Have you ever had someone bully you? What happened?

_____

_____

_____

_____

_____

2 Have you ever had to make a difficult choice when you were afraid? Explain.

_____

_____

_____

_____

_____

3 List one or more things you can do to feel better when you are afraid.

_____

_____

_____

_____

_____

My Emotions: Fear

Think about Quinn and her choice to stand up to Regina. Write about your experience being afraid and what you have learned. Did you face your fear?

Understanding the Emotion:
Frustration

Summary

In this unit, students will read a story about a fifth grader named Omar who works hard to get perfect grades. When his teacher pairs him with Landon for a science project, Omar gets frustrated because he doesn't have control over the entire assignment. When it's time to turn in the project, Omar has to make an important choice.

Class Discussion

Spend a few minutes discussing the social-emotional vocabulary for this unit. Write the word *frustrated* on the board. Ask students to define the word for you, then write their responses on the board. If time permits, have students share their prior knowledge and experience with the class regarding this emotion.

Tell students that everyone gets frustrated. When we expect things to go a certain way and they don't or when we find learning a new skill to be really difficult, we often get frustrated. Our bodies will react to this emotion. We might feel hot as our hearts beat faster. Our hands get sweaty. Our bodies tense up and we might clench our jaws. The best way to deal with this emotion is to find ways to calm down. This will help us refocus on the activity with less frustration.

Tell students that they will be reading a story about a boy who is frustrated when working on a group project. Read the story (pages 36–37) aloud or distribute copies of the story to students to read on their own. Have students choose an ending (page 38) either as a group or individually. (See page 4 for additional ideas for working with the stories and endings.)

Coping Skill Activity

Grounding exercises are similar to focused breathing. Helping children feel grounded when they are feeling big emotions like frustration is an excellent way to calm them quickly. The tree grounding meditation is a simple one that benefits both children and adults! Tell students to pretend they are trees. Have them firmly plant their feet shoulder width apart. Then tell students to firm up their tree trunks (bodies) by holding their breath and tightening all their muscles, making fists, and even tightening their faces. Then let all the tension go with a big exhale. Have them sway and shake their tree branches (arms) and feel all the energy and tension flow through their roots (feet) and into the ground. Once students have mastered the tree grounding exercise, tell them that they can practice this skill when they are feeling frustrated. When they release all their energy into the ground, have them picture the thing that is frustrating them being let go of and taken deep into the ground. Tell students they can teach this grounding exercise to their families and friends if they catch them feeling frustrated. (See page 78 for a bonus poster illustrating tree grounding.)

Personal Application

Have students come together as a whole group or in small groups to answer the discussion questions verbally. To conclude the unit, assign the written-response questions and the journal prompt as a way for students to relate the story to their own understanding of feeling frustration and how they have dealt with this emotion in their lives or have seen someone overcome this emotion.

The Group Project

"Great job on this math quiz, class. We even had a few students who scored 100%. Studying really pays off," Mr. Holton said as he walked around the classroom handing out the graded math quizzes.

Omar felt a little rush of excitement like he did every time he got a test score back. He worked extremely hard on all his assignments and studying was important to him. Mr. Holton placed Omar's quiz facedown on his desk, and Omar took a deep breath and then flipped it over to see the score. His face beamed when he saw the 100% scrawled in red pen at the top of the paper. Omar felt proud of his work and was excited to take the quiz home to show his stepdad, who had helped him study this week.

"Okay, listen up class," Mr. Holton said. "Our science lesson this week is going to be a little different. I am going to divide the class into pairs and give each pair a topic. There will be a research section, an experiment, and a short essay to write about the results. You will have time in class to deliberate with your partner and divide the work equally. Pay attention to the word *equally*. I do not want one person completing all the work, as that will result in a lower score. You are learning to collaborate and work together, which is an important percentage of your score. I am going to display the list of groups and your topics. You will have the next hour to work together to set up a plan."

Omar felt nervous as he waited for Mr. Holton to assign partners. He glanced over at his best friend, Carter, who flashed him a fingers-crossed sign as they both smiled. Carter was Omar's competition for the top grades in the class, but they were also best friends, so it was an enjoyable battle. Omar had worked on group projects with Carter before, and they loved studying and doing research together after school.

Mr. Holton projected his notes on a screen for the students to see. There were columns listing the partners and their assigned projects. Omar saw Carter's name first and his heart sank when he saw that Carter had been assigned to work with Jasmin. Their experiment was tracing constellations, which Omar thought sounded really exciting. Finally, at the bottom of the list, he found his name. He would be partnered with Landon and doing research on soil.

Omar felt the frustration start to rise inside of him as his body grew tense and irritated. This was so unfair! He looked over at Landon, who wasn't even looking at the screen and was sitting at his desk drawing cartoons.

Omar sighed and walked over to Landon's desk. "Hey, Landon, it looks like we're partners," Omar said.

Landon glanced up at the screen. "We are studying dirt. That sounds fun," he said sarcastically.

"Yeah, well I want to get a good score, so let's make a plan," Omar said with annoyance. Landon spent more time drawing his comics than he did doing homework.

Landon looked at Omar and said, "Whatever you want to do is fine by me." He put his head down and focused on his drawings.

"Ugh," Omar groaned. He sat down at the desk next to Landon's and spent the next hour compiling a list of tasks and supplies for the experiment. When Mr. Holton dismissed the class for lunch, Landon didn't even ask to see Omar's notes. He just walked out of the classroom.

The Group Project (cont.)

Omar marched home from school that day as the frustrated thoughts swirled in his head. Landon was the worst partner ever. He didn't care about schoolwork, and Omar didn't trust him to do his portion of the project. He was annoyed that Mr. Holton would partner him with Landon. Didn't he know that the two of them would not be able to work together? The frustration bubbling inside of him put Omar in a bad mood, and by the time he reached his house, he was fuming. He slammed the front door and slumped onto the couch.

"Hey Omar, what's the matter?" his stepdad asked as he found Omar on the couch. "Did you get your math quiz back today?" Omar brightened a little and handed the quiz to his stepdad. "Way to go, buddy! You didn't miss a single point. I am so proud of you," his stepdad cheered.

Omar smiled at his stepdad's enthusiasm but then replied solemnly, "I was having the best day until Mr. Holton assigned a group science project. I have to study soil and he paired me with Landon, who isn't going to work hard at all. Plus, I don't think Landon likes me. I want to do the entire project by myself so that he can't mess it up."

Omar's stepdad frowned. "I don't think that's the goal of the project. You're supposed to complete it together with Landon. Why don't you invite him over after school tomorrow?"

Omar shrugged. "We'll see," he said glumly. The last thing Omar wanted to do was invite Landon over to his house.

The next day at school, Mr. Holton assigned the class time to work on their science projects. Omar sat next to Landon and showed him his ideas for the project. Landon looked over them and disinterestedly murmured, "Looks good to me."

Omar felt exasperated and the frustration made his body feel tense. He wanted to explode and just yell at Landon to do something! Omar snapped angrily, "What part do you want to complete?"

Landon looked offended at Omar's tone but replied quietly, "Why don't I do the final essay portion at the end? I will do it tonight and we can turn everything in together tomorrow."

Omar rolled his eyes and thought to himself, "No way," but he nodded his head in agreement and then sat back at his desk to finish the research notes.

That night, Omar finished his portion of the assignment but worried about Landon's essay. Omar felt bad for snapping at Landon out of frustration. He thought about calling Landon to see how the essay writing was going, but instead he sat back at his desk and wrote the essay himself. He figured it would be better to have a backup plan just in case Landon didn't complete the essay.

At school the next day, Landon handed his essay portion to Omar and smiled. "Here you go. I am sure we'll get a good grade."

Omar looked at Landon inquisitively. He thanked him and took the essay. As he went to staple it to his portion of the assignment, he hesitated. He remembered he still had his essay portion in his backpack, and he felt certain that it was better than Landon's work.

Should Omar turn in his own essay instead of Landon's essay?

©Teacher Created Resources

Making Choices

Choice 1—Yes

Omar cared about his grade and the idea of getting a bad score because of Landon's indifference was too much for him to bear. He placed Landon's essay in his desk and stapled his own essay to the final project before handing it in to Mr. Holton. Omar sat at his desk and breathed a sigh of relief. He was certain they would get a good grade on the project.

The next day at school, Mr. Holton finished the math lesson and asked Landon and Omar to stay for a moment to speak with him before he dismissed the rest of the class to recess. Landon gave Omar a confused look. They both approached Mr. Holton's desk as he handed them back their project. "Please explain to me how this project was a collaboration," Mr. Holton said sternly.

Landon looked puzzled and replied, "Omar did the research and the experiment, and I wrote the final essay."

Mr. Holton showed the essay to Landon and stated, "Landon, I know enough to know that this is not your handwriting."

Landon glanced at the paper and then shot Omar an angry look. "Ugh! It was hard enough to be your partner! You couldn't even turn in my work?" Landon yelled.

Omar's face burned red. He didn't even know how to explain his actions. "Mr. Holton, it was hard for me to partner with Landon and I was feeling frustrated. I just wanted our grade to be perfect," Omar mumbled.

"Where is Landon's essay?" Mr. Holton demanded. Omar retrieved the essay from his desk and handed it to his teacher. "I will regrade your science project using this essay. Landon, you may go to recess. Omar, you need to join me on a trip to the principal's office to schedule a conference with your parents about this." Omar turned to Landon and apologized before quietly following Mr. Holton to the office.

Choice 2—No

Omar held Landon's essay in his hands and paused before stapling it to his own portion. He didn't have time to read it, but it looked like Landon wrote a decent essay. He wondered if it was as good as his own. Omar felt frustrated that his own grade was half-determined by someone else's work. That didn't seem fair to him at all. Then he remembered Mr. Holton saying that the point of the project was teamwork.

Omar closed his eyes and took a deep breath as he pondered his choices. He opened his eyes and stapled Landon's essay to his portion before turning it in.

The next day, Mr. Holton told the students to sit next to their partners so that he could distribute the graded science projects. Landon sat next to Omar, and Mr. Holton handed them their project. Omar was nervous to look at the score, but Landon smiled and said, "Good work, teammate. We got a 95%."

Omar breathed a sigh of relief. "I'm sorry for getting frustrated with you," he said softly. "It just means a lot to me to get good grades."

Landon shrugged his shoulders and replied, "I know it wasn't easy to work with me. I was nervous about working with you because you want everything to be perfect. But I really tried my hardest so that you would be happy."

Omar smiled at Landon with appreciation. "Next time, I will be a less controlling partner."

What Do You Think?

Choice 1

1 Why do you think Omar didn't trust Landon's essay?

2 How do you think Landon felt when he found out what Omar did?

3 What lesson did Omar learn?

4 Do you think Omar will handle group projects differently in the future?

Choice 2

1 What did Omar do to calm his frustration?

2 How do you think Landon felt when he saw their grade?

3 What did Omar learn about what he's like as a partner?

4 Do you think Omar will handle group projects differently in the future?

What Would You Do?

1 Have you ever felt frustrated when working on a group project? Explain.

_____

_____

_____

_____

_____

_____

2 Why do you think teachers assign group work?

_____

_____

_____

_____

_____

_____

3 List one or more things you can do to calm down when you are feeling frustrated.

_____

_____

_____

_____

My Emotions: Frustration

Think about Omar's story and his frustration over not having control over the entire project.
Write about your experience feeling frustrated and how you have learned to calm that feeling.

Understanding the Emotion:
Shyness

Summary

In this unit, students will read a story about Victoria, a fifth-grade student who moves to a new school. Victoria is extremely shy and has trouble meeting new people and trying new things. When a classmate asks her to join the afterschool art club, Victoria has to decide whether to conquer her shyness to try something new.

Class Discussion

Spend a few minutes discussing the social-emotional vocabulary for this unit. Write the word *shy* on the board. Ask students to define the word for you, then write their responses on the board. If time permits, have students share their prior knowledge and experience with the class regarding this emotion.

Remind students that most children feel shy at some time or another. Starting a new school, joining a new club, or meeting a new person are all events that might make us feel uncomfortable. But after some time, we start to warm up to people or the new situation. As we feel more comfortable, we can open up and be ourselves. This process may take longer for some children.

Tell students that they will be reading a story about a girl who is shy and has to make a choice about stepping outside of her comfort zone. Read the story (pages 42–43) aloud or distribute copies of the story to students to read on their own. Have students choose an ending (page 44) either as a group or individually. (See page 4 for additional ideas for working with the stories and endings.)

Coping Skill Activity

Partner activities work best for shy students, and repetitive practice will eventually create the safe space that these children need to feel comfortable. These students may benefit from having a rehearsed script to follow to ease their discomfort. An enjoyable game for students to play is "Would You Rather?" Tell students to stand up and ask them a question. (**For example:** Would you rather swim in the ocean or play in the snow? Would you rather be able to fly or breathe underwater? Would you rather never be able to play video games again or never watch TV again? Would you rather eat a cricket or a worm? Would you rather drink a cup of hot sauce or sour milk? Would you rather have a pet unicorn or a pet dinosaur?) Have the right side of the room represent one choice and the left side of the room represent the other choice. Students will move to the side of the room that represents their choice. Then, casually interview a few students from each side to have them explain why they made that choice. Try to alternate the interviewees each round to give every student (including the shy ones) a chance to speak out loud.

Personal Application

Have students come together as a whole group or in small groups to answer the discussion questions verbally. To conclude the unit, assign the written-response questions and the journal prompt as a way for students to relate the story to their own understanding of shyness and how they have dealt with this emotion or have seen someone overcome this emotion.

The New School

"Mom, I can't go. I don't think I can do this," Victoria sniffled. She wiped tears away from her eyes and stared out the car window. They were sitting in the parking lot of Oak Grove Elementary School, watching the students smiling and crowding the campus playground. They were all wearing winter coats and snow boots and were stomping around in the remaining patches of melting snow. It was February and the school year was halfway over, but today was Victoria's first day. She and her mother had just moved to the new town of Oak Grove. Victoria was not thrilled to have to start at a new school in the middle of the year.

Victoria had trouble meeting new people. She never felt excited for experiences that were outside of her comfort zone. She spoke softly and infrequently. She mostly enjoyed being alone and working on her art. She loved to paint and could spend hours a day sitting in front of a canvas. Victoria remembered hearing her kindergarten teacher say that Victoria was shy. She felt the word *shy* explained how uncomfortable she felt in social situations. However, despite her shyness, she made a best friend named Flora and they stuck together like glue for the next six years. Victoria's kindergarten teacher partnered them together because Flora was also quiet and shy. The girls liked sitting together and coloring and observing the chaos of the other kids around them. They both enjoyed listening to conversations more than participating. Flora made Victoria feel comfortable. But today she was about to face a new school, a new teacher, and new students without the comfort of her best friend by her side.

"Victoria, you can do this," her mother reassured her. "I know that it is difficult for you to try new things. I was exactly the same way when I was your age. I was so shy that I wouldn't even order food in a restaurant! I whispered so softly when I talked that some kids thought I couldn't speak. There isn't anything wrong with being shy. But you can't miss out on life because of it. The only way to conquer your shyness is to practice doing new things. Today is the start of so many new adventures. Each time you step outside of your comfort zone, the easier it will feel. I know you can do it."

Victoria put on her winter coat and grabbed her brand-new backpack. It was printed with Van Gogh's *Starry Night*, which was one of her favorite paintings. She took a deep breath and gave her mom a hug. Her hands were shaking, and she felt a cold sense of dread in her stomach. She stepped out of the car and approached the new school and the hordes of students running around excitedly.

Victoria tucked her hands inside her coat pockets to keep them from shaking as she approached the other students, who were starting to line up for class. She knew where her classroom was because she took a tour with her mom the night before and tried to memorize everything to make her first day less scary. Victoria disliked being the center of attention in any way and today she knew that all eyes were on her as she lined up in front of Mrs. Bennet's fifth-grade classroom. The other students turned to look at her and she could hear a few of them whisper to one another, "Who is that girl? Is she a new student?" Mrs. Bennet opened the classroom door and the students all hurried to their seats. Victoria just stood in the doorway without knowing where to sit. She felt uncomfortable and awkward as the students took their seats and continued to watch her.

The New School (cont.)

"Listen up, everyone. Today is a special day as we have a new student in our class. Her name is Victoria and she has just moved to town, so please be extra helpful in showing her around and making her feel welcome." Mrs. Bennet smiled warmly and led Victoria to an empty desk in the back of the room.

Victoria breathed a sigh of relief that she could hide in the back of the room. She took her seat and began to unpack her backpack. She pulled out her notebook and began flipping through it to find a blank page since the first few pages were already full of her drawings and doodles.

"Cool backpack. I love Van Gogh. Oh wow, those drawings are really good! Did you draw those yourself?" a voice whispered. Victoria looked over at the student sitting next to her and just nodded shyly.

"I like to draw things too. I mostly draw comics though," he said, and he lifted up his notebook to show her his artwork. Victoria smiled as she looked at it. "My name is Micah. I know you probably don't know anyone, so I can introduce you and show you around. Tomorrow after school is art club, and I am the president. We meet in this classroom and work on different art pieces every week. You should come and check it out." Victoria nodded her head and thought about how fun it would be to join an art club. Her old school didn't offer anything like that. But then she paused to think of how uncomfortable she would feel to join a club where she didn't know anyone.

The rest of the school day was a blur as Victoria followed everyone around through the different activities and tried to remain invisible. She relaxed and breathed a sigh of relief when she saw her mom's car waiting in the parking lot. Suddenly, Victoria felt a tap on her shoulder. Micah handed her a flyer and said, "This is the information for art club tomorrow. I hope you can come."

Victoria nodded and continued walking toward her car. She knew that art club would be something she would probably love, but the uncomfortable feeling of walking into a club where she had no friends made her feel shaky and nervous.

Should Victoria join the art club?

Making Choices

Choice 1—Yes

Victoria felt an abundance of relief as she hopped into the car and hugged her mom. "I survived my first day at Oak Grove Elementary," she said with a reluctant smile.

Her mom's face lit up as she said, "I knew everything would turn out fine. Tomorrow will be even easier. Remember that it just takes some practice."

Victoria nodded and handed her mom the flyer for the art club. She murmured softly, "I was asked to join this club, but I'm unsure about it. What do you think?"

Her mom read the flyer and exclaimed excitedly, "Victoria, this club sounds like it was designed for you! Did you read what they do? Each week is a new art media. Tomorrow is sculpting. You just said the other day you wanted to try sculpting! This club is practically perfect. Why wouldn't you want to join?"

Victoria shifted in her seat nervously and looked at her mom. "I know it *sounds* perfect, but I don't feel comfortable joining a club where I don't know anyone. That part sounds miserable."

Victoria's mom placed her hand on Victoria's back reassuringly and replied, "You will never know unless you try. Why don't you at least go to one session and see how it feels?" Victoria took a deep breath and nodded her head in agreement.

The next day at school was easier than the first and the routine of the day was feeling more familiar. After school, Micah ran up to Victoria excitedly and said, "You are coming to art club today, right?" She nodded. "Okay, do you want to help me set things up?" he asked.

She smiled and followed Micah into the classroom. They unpacked huge blocks of clay and set up a table in the back of the room for sculpting. Victoria relaxed when she saw that art club was only five other students. They spent the hour working on their individual sculptures, and Victoria loved every minute of it. She realized that she had found her new place of comfort.

Choice 2—No

Victoria stuffed the art club flyer in her backpack and hurriedly raced to hop into her mom's car. "So, was it as awful as you imagined it would be?" her mom teased.

Victoria smiled and said, "It was scary and uncomfortable, and I am glad it is over. I do hope tomorrow will be easier."

"Did you meet any new friends?" her mom inquired gently.

Victoria thought about Micah and the art club but hesitated. She didn't want to tell her mom about the art club because she didn't feel ready to join it. "Everyone was nice to me," Victoria said quietly.

The next day at school, Micah asked Victoria if she was going to come to art club. She shook her head no and said, "I have plans after school today."

Micah looked disappointed and instantly Victoria felt bad for lying. But the unknown made her uncomfortable and she had never been in an art club before.

On Wednesday morning, Victoria found her seat in the classroom and was astonished to see a table in the back of the room displaying different half-finished clay sculptures. She had just told her mom the other day that she wanted to try sculpting. She was sorry she hadn't had the chance to try it.

Micah saw her eyeing the statues and whispered, "That is what we started yesterday in art club. We could really use some help if you want to come next week." Victoria took a deep breath and told him she would be there.

What Do You Think?

Choice 1

1. Do you think Victoria was excited to join the art club?

2. Do you think Victoria will always feel shy?

3. Why do you think Victoria's mom told her that practicing would help her feel more comfortable?

4. Do you think Victoria will find it easier to try new things after her experience at her new school?

Choice 2

1. Why did Victoria not tell her mom about art club?

2. How do you think Micah felt when Victoria didn't come to art club?

3. Do you think Victoria will enjoy art club?

4. Do you think Victoria will always find it hard to try something new?

What Would You Do?

1. Can you think of a time you felt shy or too uncomfortable to try something new? What did you do?

_____

_____

_____

_____

_____

2. Have you ever had to attend a new school? What was your experience like? If you haven't had to do that, how do you imagine it would be?

_____

_____

_____

_____

_____

3. List one or more things you can do to help you feel brave when you are feeling shy.

_____

_____

_____

_____

_____

My Emotions: Shyness

Think about Victoria's story. Have you ever felt shy? Or do you know someone who is shy? Write about your experience and what you have learned.

Understanding the Emotion:
Jealousy

Summary

In this unit, students will read a story about Wyatt, whose mother is remarried and has just had a new baby. Wyatt struggles with feeling jealous over all the attention the new baby is getting as he tries to figure out where he fits in the new family unit.

Class Discussion

Spend a few minutes discussing the social-emotional vocabulary for this unit. Write the word *jealous* on the board. Ask students to define the word for you, then write their responses on the board. If time permits, have students share their prior knowledge and experience with the class regarding this emotion.

Tell students that everyone feels jealous at times. We might feel jealous of a baby brother or sister because they seem to get more attention. We can be jealous if someone has something we want, like a new bike or a new pet, or is better at something than we are, such as a sport or a school subject. We can also feel jealous if our best friend spends a lot of time with a new friend. Jealousy may make us feel angry or sad. Reassure students that feeling jealous is normal but there are things we can do to help calm this emotion.

Tell students that they will be reading a story about a boy who is jealous of his new baby sister and has to make a choice when dealing with this emotion. Read the story (pages 48–49) aloud or distribute copies of the story to students to read on their own. Have students choose an ending (page 50) either as a group or individually. (See page 4 for additional ideas for working with the stories and endings.)

Coping Skill Activity

Jealousy can always be reversed with gratitude. If we remember the things we have that we are grateful for, our jealous feelings will subside. Give each student three index cards or small squares of paper. Have them write down three things that they are thankful for in their lives. It can be positive things about themselves, people they are happy to know, or even items that they own that make them happy. Tape these to their tables or desks and tell students that when they are feeling jealous, they can read the reminders of the things that they do have in their lives. Encourage students to do the same thing at home so they can feel grateful for the positive things instead of dwelling on the negative emotion of jealousy.

Personal Application

Have students come together as a whole group or in small groups to answer the discussion questions verbally. To conclude the unit, assign the written-response questions and the journal prompt as a way for students to relate the story to their own understanding of feeling jealous and how they have dealt with this emotion in their lives.

A New Family

"Aren't you excited about our new baby sister? Your mom is bringing her home today! My dad just called and texted me photos. Look how adorable she is!" Kayla squealed with delight.

But her stepbrother Wyatt just shrugged and said, "She's just a baby. She can't do anything but eat and sleep. We'll have to clean up after her and change her diapers. Why would I be excited? It's just more chaos in this already chaotic new life."

Kayla's smile left her face and she said softly, "I like our new life. Your mom is really nice to me, and I don't care if you don't help with the baby. I'll take care of her." Kayla stood up and went into the kitchen to get a snack.

Wyatt sighed and felt a little bad for hurting Kayla's feelings, but he was so tired of hearing about the baby and how excited he was supposed to feel when he just felt angry and jealous. His mom married Kayla's dad a year ago, and Wyatt was still getting used to their new home and having Kayla as a sister. And for the last nine months, his mom had been completely focused on the arrival of the new baby. She spent all her time buying new things for the baby and decorating the nursery. New gifts arrived in the mail every day for the baby, but nothing came for Wyatt. This baby was already stealing the last remaining bits of attention he could get from his mom, and he resented the baby before she even arrived.

Kayla came back in the room and took a big bite out of her apple as she stared at Wyatt. "I think you're just jealous," she stated. "You want to be the center of attention and you always were, and this is finally the one time you aren't, and you don't like it. I know how you feel. I was jealous of you for a long time because my dad always talked about how excited he was to finally have a son. But when I told him that I felt jealous, he reminded me that everyone feels jealous at times and that I should focus on all the things that make me so special, like how I always beat you at video games," Kayla teased. She handed a video game controller to Wyatt.

He took the controller and murmured, "Game on," but he had a hard time focusing on the game. He thought about Kayla's allegation that he was jealous, but it only made him feel mad. Why couldn't anyone understand that this whole situation was so unfair to him? He had no control over anything, and nobody ever asked what he wanted. They just expected him to be happy and excited about everything.

"Wyatt and Kayla, come meet your new baby sister," Kayla's dad whispered as he carried a tiny round basket into the house. Wyatt's mom followed, her face glowing with happiness.

Kayla whispered in a high-pitched tone, "I have the cutest baby sister in the whole wide world!"

Wyatt rolled his eyes and muttered, "Are we all using baby voices now?"

Wyatt's mom shot him a stern look and said, "Please, no attitude today, Wyatt." She walked over to him and gave him a big hug. "I missed you while I was in the hospital. I know that you are not thrilled about having a baby sister, but I really hope you will at least try to spend time with her. That's all I ask of you."

A New Family (cont.)

She took the tiny baby out of the car seat and showed them how to hold her. Kayla jumped at the chance and immediately held the baby gently in her arms. "She's sleeping right now, but if she cries, she usually calms down as soon as you hold her," Wyatt's mom said as she gazed with adoration at the tiny baby. Then she yawned and declared, "I am going upstairs to take a nap. Will you two help watch over her?" Kayla agreed enthusiastically, but Wyatt just shrugged his shoulders.

Wyatt watched his mom head off to bed, and as he looked at Kayla and her dad cooing over the baby, he felt the jealousy rise up and explode. He felt so misplaced in this new family and he just wanted things to go back to the way they were before. The jealous feeling turned into rage as Wyatt threw down his video game controller and shouted, "I have better things to do with my time than to help with the baby!" He walked briskly to his bedroom and slammed the door hard.

The loud thud of the door slamming woke up the baby and she started to cry. Wyatt heard the wailing cries through his bedroom door. He felt bad about waking the baby, but then he heard Kayla singing soothing songs to the baby and her dad preparing a bottle, and he was determined to have no part in it. After a few minutes, the wailing cries stopped. Wyatt mumbled to himself, "Finally, we have some peace," and spent the next hour playing video games in his room.

Later that afternoon, he heard Kayla's mom arrive to pick her up for the weekend, and he peeked through his bedroom window and watched them drive off. He wished he had said goodbye to her and suddenly realized that Kayla was the one thing he was most grateful for in his life right now. She wanted to be his sister, and he enjoyed spending time with her. Wyatt thought about Kayla's method of coping with jealousy and wondered if he should try it too.

Just then, he heard his baby sister's cries coming from the kitchen. When he ventured out of his room, he heard his mom upstairs in the shower and his stepdad fast asleep on the couch. His new baby sister was fussing and crying in her tiny bassinet in the kitchen. Wyatt peered down at her and was astonished when she looked right back at him and wailed louder. He knew he should probably try to comfort her but remembered his declaration that he would have no part in helping with the baby.

Should Wyatt help calm the baby?

Making Choices

Choice 1—Yes

Wyatt stared at his tiny baby sister as she fussed, grunted, stretched, and cried, and he realized that she had no control over this new life either. His heart immediately softened. "Do you feel lost being in this new place too? I can definitely relate to that," he whispered soothingly. The baby's fussing grew quieter as she tried to focus her gaze onto Wyatt. He gently slid one arm underneath her body and the other hand behind her head and lifted her out of her bassinet. He sat down on the floor and held her close as he looked down at her tiny body.

Wyatt sweetly sang a lullaby he remembered his mother singing to him when he was younger. The baby sighed deeply, yawned, and fell back to sleep. "I did it!" Wyatt whispered to himself excitedly. "I helped her fall back asleep."

Just then his mom rushed into the kitchen, her hair still wet from her shower. "I heard her crying and was concerned…." Her voice trailed off as she saw Wyatt cuddling with his baby sister. Wyatt's mom's face beamed with happiness and she sat down next to him on the kitchen floor. "Thank you so much for helping to calm her. I am sure she loves you and is going to adore having you as her big brother just as much as Kayla does."

Wyatt smiled and felt the jealousy ease inside of him. He did have a unique place in this new family, and he realized he felt grateful for every one of his new family members.

Choice 2—No

Wyatt stared at his tiny baby sister as she wailed louder in the bassinet. He heard his mom turn off the shower, and the jealousy bubbled up inside of him. It wasn't fair that this teeny tiny baby was the center of everyone's world, and he was lingering on the outside without any attention. Wyatt heard his mom's footsteps hurrying down the stairs before she rushed into the room and saw Wyatt glaring at the crying baby.

"Oh, Wyatt," his mother sighed with exasperation. "She simply wants to be held. Would you like to hold her?"

Wyatt defiantly shook his head no and returned to his bedroom as his mom calmed the screaming baby. A few minutes later, he heard a gentle knock on his door and his mom came in holding the baby in one arm and a gift in the other.

"More gifts for the baby?" Wyatt asked, rolling his eyes.

"No, Wyatt. This one is for you from me and your stepdad. We wanted to say thank you for helping to watch Kayla while I was in the hospital."

Wyatt looked confused. "I get a gift for that? But she's my sister, and we have fun hanging out."

His mom smiled at that comment, and Wyatt realized that this baby was his sister too. He unwrapped the gift and was thrilled to see it was a new video game. "Thank you, Mom. I am sorry for letting the jealousy control me. I am genuinely grateful to be in this family. Can I hold her?" he asked, and his mom softly handed him the baby. "Welcome to our family," Wyatt whispered soothingly as the baby snuggled in his arms.

#8314 *What Would YOU Do?*

What Do You Think?

Choice 1

1. How did Wyatt relate to the baby?

2. How do you think Wyatt felt when he helped his baby sister stop crying?

3. How do you think Wyatt's mom felt when she saw him holding the baby?

4. What did Wyatt learn about feeling jealous?

Choice 2

1. Why did Wyatt feel jealous of the baby?

2. How did talking to his mom help Wyatt feel better?

3. Do you think Wyatt will help out more with the baby?

4. What did Wyatt learn about feeling jealous?

©Teacher Created Resources

#8314 What Would YOU Do?

What Would You Do?

1 How would you feel if you had a new baby sibling?

_____

_____

_____

_____

_____

2 Have you ever made a bad choice because you were jealous? What happened?

_____

_____

_____

_____

_____

3 List one or more things you can do to feel better when you are feeling jealous.

_____

_____

_____

_____

_____

My Emotions: Jealousy

Think about Wyatt's story. Have you ever felt jealous? Write about your experience and what you have learned.

Understanding the Emotion: Anxiety

Summary

In this unit, students will read a story about a girl named Michelle who feels anxiety about sleeping away from home. When her sixth-grade class signs up for science camp, Michelle has to make a choice to conquer her anxiety and go or stay home and miss out on science camp.

Class Discussion

Spend a few minutes discussing the social-emotional vocabulary for this unit. Write the word *anxious* on the board. Ask students to define the word for you, then write their responses on the board. If time permits, have students share their prior knowledge and experience with the class regarding this emotion.

Remind students that everyone has things that make them anxious. It could be meeting new people or going to new places. Needles, doctor's offices, and hospitals are a common source of anxiety for people. Spending the night away from home is also a common cause of anxiety. The best way to feel less anxious is to practice the things that make you feel anxious until they become more comfortable. Deep breathing exercises can help calm your body when you know you are going to be in an anxious situation.

Tell students that they will be reading a story about a child who is anxious about sleeping away from home and has to make a choice. Read the story (pages 54–55) aloud or distribute copies of the story to students to read on their own. Have students choose an ending (page 56) either as a group or individually. (See page 4 for additional ideas for working with the stories and endings.)

Coping Skill Activity

Learning to calm our anxiety through our breathing is a fantastic skill to master because we can do it anywhere. Shape tracing while breathing helps kids focus their minds as they breathe. You can have students draw simple shapes to trace on paper, or have them use their index fingers to trace shapes on their legs. Any shape with sides will work. So, for example, have students practice tracing a square on their leg. They will draw one side as they breathe in deeply, hold at the point, then exhale slowly for the next side, and repeat as they trace the square. They can do the same with a triangle or a star. Remind students that they are to be breathing deeply, as this kind of breathing will slow down their heart rate and help them feel calmer. (See page 80 for a bonus poster illustrating shape breathing.)

Personal Application

Have students come together as a whole group or in small groups to answer the discussion questions verbally. To conclude the unit, assign the written-response questions and the journal writing as a way for students to relate the story to their own understanding of feeling anxiety and how they have dealt with this emotion in their lives or have seen someone overcome this emotion.

Sixth-Grade Science Camp

"Listen up, students! This is what you all have been waiting for, I know. Next week, our sixth-grade class will be attending outdoor education. We will spend four days at Starry Nights Ranch, and you can sign up on your permission slip for who you want to be your cabin bunkmate. There's a list of all the supplies you will need to pack in your duffel bags, including a sleeping bag and pillow. Oh, and remember to pack a flashlight. The night hike on astronomy night is marvelous. This is my favorite week of the school year, and I know you all are going to love it!" Mrs. Morrison grinned at the class.

The students burst into excited chatter and turned to one another to look for possible bunkmates as Mrs. Morrison handed out the permission slips. But Michelle sat still in her seat, the cold dread of anxiety making her feel dizzy. Her palms were sweaty, and she rubbed them on her jeans and tried to calm her racing heart. Her best friend, Sara, turned to her and beamed. "Michelle, will you be my bunkmate? This is going to be awesome! We can go on hikes and sing songs at the campfire and tell silly stories from our sleeping bags. As soon as Mrs. Morrison said astronomy night, I knew you would be thrilled!" Sara exclaimed enthusiastically.

Michelle managed to nod and summoned up a tiny smile. But she could not stop the racing thoughts of dread in her head. She stuffed the permission slip into her backpack and rested her head on her desk.

Michelle had tried sleeping away from home one time when she was eight years old. It was at her cousin Jayne's house, and she didn't even last the whole night. As soon as it was time to go to sleep, she felt anxious. She missed her parents and her own bed. The worrying thoughts made her sick to her stomach, and eventually she called her parents to come pick her up at midnight. Her parents believed she just had a stomach virus, but Michelle had felt better as soon as she was back home in her own bed. She never told her parents that she was feeling anxiety about being away from home. Ever since that night, Michelle came up with excuses for why she couldn't sleep over at Sara's house, and she never tried spending the night at her cousin's house again, despite all of Jayne's persistent pleas.

That night at home, Michelle pulled the crumpled-up permission slip out from her backpack and stared at it. With a heavy sigh, she handed it to her mom. Michelle's mom's face lit up as she filled out the permission slip. Then she exclaimed with a giddy voice, "Sixth-grade science camp! How exciting! I went when I was in sixth grade too, and it was the best week of my elementary-school career."

Michelle mumbled, "That seems to be what everyone says about it," as she stuffed the permission slip back in her backpack.

The next day at school, all the kids in Michelle's class were buzzing around and talking nonstop about going to sixth-grade camp. Sara told Michelle that she bought a brand-new sleeping bag that had a purple and blue tie-dye print. Then she opened her backpack, pulled out a sparkly green flashlight, and handed it to Michelle. "I bought this flashlight for you! My mom and I saw it while we were shopping at the store last night, and we instantly thought of you because you love green so much. I got a sparkly purple one, and I thought they would be perfect for our night hike."

Sixth-Grade Science Camp *(cont.)*

Michelle smiled sadly. "Thank you, Sara," she said softly as she studied the flashlight in her hand. She knew that camp was going to be as amazing as everyone said it was, but she couldn't stop the anxious thoughts from spinning in her head. What if she felt sick again, and what would she do if she couldn't sleep? The camp was hours away and it wasn't like she could just have her mom come get her in the middle of the night.

Michelle felt herself grow anxious as she imagined the embarrassment of having her mom come pick her up from camp. There was no way she could go. The anxiety was making her feel sick already. She wrapped her arms tightly around her stomach to ease the churning sensation.

"Hey, what's the matter?" Sara asked gently when she saw the look of concern on Michelle's face. "Science camp totally sounds like something you would love, and you haven't seemed excited at all. You read all those astronomy books and you even own a telescope! You know more about the stars than anyone I've ever known. Oh, and I heard that there's an ice cream sundae night. How great is that?"

Michelle took a deep breath and tried to steady her shaking hands. She felt self-conscious about her anxiety and didn't know how to talk about it. "I have never spent the night away from home," Michelle stammered.

She was expecting Sara to laugh, but instead Sara gave her a big hug and said, "I know how that feels! I get nervous about being away too, but we will have each other! We can share a cabin and it will be just like any other day, only we get to sleep in a new place. If you feel scared or nervous or anxious, you can talk to me and I will help you." Sara smiled. "Please come to camp because I don't want to go without you!" Michelle hugged Sara back, thanked her for her support, and agreed to go to camp.

The days flew by and it suddenly it was Monday morning. Michelle woke up early to the sound of her alarm clock beeping steadily. She rubbed her eyes and sat up in bed. But when she saw her sleeping bag and packed duffle bag waiting in the corner of the room, her heart dropped into her stomach. She felt the dizzy swirl of anxiety in her head and she crawled back in bed underneath her covers. She didn't think she would be able to go. She wanted to tell her parents that she woke up feeling unwell. But she didn't want to upset Sara by staying home.

Should Michelle go to science camp?

Making Choices

Choice 1-Yes

Michelle took a deep breath as she stared at her packed bags. She tried to calm her pounding heart with slow, steady breathing. Her mom came in to make sure she was awake and saw her still in bed. "Michelle, are you feeling okay?" her mom asked with concern. Michelle nodded her head and told her mom that she was feeling anxious about going to camp.

Michelle's mom gave her a hug and reminded her that everything was going to be okay. "I remember feeling anxious about science camp too. I was worried that I wouldn't like the food and I would miss my parents too much. But once I was there, camp turned out to be so full of exciting activities that the days flew by. Your teacher sent me an email saying that she will send us photos and we can write you letters back. I think I will miss you more than you will miss me," Michelle's mom chuckled.

Michelle felt her body relax, and she hugged her mom tightly before she jumped up and got ready for the trip. She felt anxious again when they pulled up to school and saw the school bus waiting and all the sixth graders lined up with their gear, but Michelle focused on breathing deeply. She clutched her sleeping bag and stepped out of the car. She immediately found Sara, and they rode on the bus together. The students sang silly songs on the bus, and the drive went by quickly.

When the bus pulled up to the camp, Michelle smiled at the sight of a huge telescope set up in a field. Sara and Michelle dropped off their bags in their little wooden cabin, and Michelle paused to exclaim, "I am so glad we're here! This place is amazing!" Then the girls skipped toward the picnic tables for their first meal together at camp.

Choice 2-No

Michelle's heart was racing, and she felt dizzy. She crawled back into her bed and let the anxiety cloud her thoughts. Her mom came in, saw her still in bed, and asked, "Michelle, are you feeling okay?"

Michelle realized that this was her chance and she moaned, "No, I woke up feeling awful and don't think I can go to camp."

Her mom looked worried and sat down on her bed. "Where do you feel sick, Michelle?" she asked.

Michelle tried to think of a convincing lie and stammered, "My stomach is upset, my head hurts, and I think I am going to throw up."

Michelle's mom frowned and said, "I am so sorry, Michelle. I will call the school and tell them you have to miss camp." Michelle nodded and squeezed her pillow tightly as she closed her eyes. The day dragged on so slowly, and Michelle stayed in bed all day but was extremely bored. She wondered if she made the right choice or if she should have gone to science camp.

That night, her mom knocked on her door and told Michelle she had something special to show her. The students at camp sent an email to Michelle's mom with photos of them holding "Get Well" signs that they made and photos of activities they were doing at camp. There was a photo of Sara in a cabin that she was sharing with one of the camp leaders. Michelle felt awful for lying about being sick and wondered if Sara was going to be upset with her. Seeing all the kids at the camp doing fun things made her realize that she was missing out on making exciting memories and she wished that she had chosen to go.

What Do You Think?

Choice 1

1. Do you think talking to her mom helped Michelle?

2. What did Michelle do to help calm her anxiety?

3. Do you think Sara was happy to see that Michelle showed up?

4. Do you think Michelle will feel less anxiety about sleepovers after going to camp?

Choice 2

1. Why did Michelle feel anxious about going to camp?

2. Why did Michelle lie and say she was sick?

3. How do you think Sara felt when Michelle didn't show up for school that day?

4. What was something Michelle could have done to help lessen her anxiety?

What Would You Do?

1 Have you ever felt anxious about sleeping away from home? Write about it.

_____

_____

_____

_____

_____

2 Would you be able to go to sleepover camp if you were feeling anxious? Explain.

_____

_____

_____

_____

_____

3 List one or more things you can do to calm down when you are feeling anxious.

_____

_____

_____

_____

_____

My Emotions: Anxiety

Think about Michelle's story. Have you ever felt anxious about something? Write about your experience and what you have learned.

Understanding the Emotion: Embarrassment

Summary

In this unit, students will read a story about a girl named Izzy whose dad loses his job and whose family is living on a tight financial budget. Izzy feels embarrassed when she can't afford to buy things with her friends at the mall. She has to make a choice whether to steal an item or confess that she doesn't have the money.

Class Discussion

Spend a few minutes discussing the social-emotional vocabulary for this unit. Write the word *embarrassed* on the board. Ask students to define the word for you, then write their responses on the board. If time permits, have students share their prior knowledge and experience with the class regarding this emotion.

Tell students that everyone has felt embarrassed for many different reasons, such as not having a lot of money, not speaking a language well or speaking it with an accent, or being too short or too tall. We have all tripped, spilled something, or stumbled over our words when speaking in public. The feeling of embarrassment might make our cheeks feel hot and red or our bodies shaky. The important thing to remember is that those moments affect us more than the people who saw the embarrassing moment. If we do something embarrassing, we might think about it over and over. But chances are, no one else will! The best way to let go of this feeling is to accept what it is and move on! Talking about our embarrassment is a great way to feel better. Our friends or family members might share a similar experience. Also, it is best to not hide from embarrassment. You never want to give up on things you enjoy or make decisions just because you are afraid of being embarrassed.

Tell students that they will be reading a story about a girl who feels embarrassed for not having enough money and has to make a choice when dealing with this emotion. Read the story (pages 60–61) aloud or distribute copies of the story to students to read on their own. Have students choose an ending (page 62) either as a group or individually. (See page 4 for additional ideas for working with the stories and endings.)

Coping Skill Activity

Sometimes, we replay an embarrassing moment over and over in our heads. This will only make us feel worse. Distraction coping skills can help us take our mind off of the event. Tell students that there are many different distraction coping skills they can use if they need to stop thinking about the moment. Have students practice a few different distraction coping skills to see which one works best for them.

- Tell a few jokes or read a funny story
- Go for a jog
- Make a list of ten good things about yourself
- Sing a song

Personal Application

Have students come together as a whole group or in small groups to answer the discussion questions verbally. To conclude the unit, assign the written-response questions and the journal prompt as a way for students to relate the story to their own understanding of feeling embarrassed and how they have dealt with this emotion in their lives.

The Shopping Trip

"Hey Mom, I'm home from school," Izzy yelled loudly as she darted through the front door and dropped her backpack in the hallway. She ventured into the kitchen to grab a snack and was surprised to see her father drinking a cup of tea at the kitchen table. "Dad, you're home early! You can help me finish my science homework tonight. This will be perfect!" Izzy ran over to give her dad a big hug.

"Well, Izzy, I will be home more lately, because the business I work at closed today, and I don't have a job there anymore. I will help you with your homework while I look for a new job," he said.

Izzy searched his face to see if he was upset, but her dad seemed calm. "Dad, is everything going to be okay? Are you upset?" she asked.

He smiled and answered, "Everything will be fine, and I am not upset. I will find another job soon enough, however, we will be on a very tight budget until I do."

Izzy stared at him with a confused look and said, "What is a budget?" Izzy's dad cleared his throat and said, "To begin with, we can't pay you an allowance anymore. We have to be extremely smart about how we spend our money. We will save money by eating meals at home and not spending as much money on entertainment, like going to the movies or arcades."

"No allowance at all?" Izzy groaned. "But this weekend I am going to the mall with Harper and Bailey, and I only have four dollars in my wallet."

Her father gave her a stern look and replied, "Well, that four dollars is yours to spend wisely. But it's all you get for now."

Izzy made herself a snack of cheese and crackers and sat down next to her dad at the table. She tried to do her science homework but kept getting distracted by thoughts about her dad's unemployment. What would happen to them if he couldn't find a job? Would they have to move? Izzy loved their house and their neighborhood. She never really worried about money before but now she felt concerned. What would she tell Harper and Bailey? She felt her face flush red with embarrassment. She didn't want to tell them that she couldn't go to the mall because she didn't have any money.

Izzy's mom came into the kitchen and patted Izzy on the back reassuringly. "Everything is going to be fine, Izzy. We are not defined by our income, which means that money isn't everything. Our happiness comes from better sources, like one another!" She chuckled as she playfully ruffled Izzy's hair. Izzy smiled back at her mom but still felt a lingering dread about telling her friends about her new budget.

On Saturday morning, Harper's mom drove up to Izzy's house and honked the car horn. Izzy shoved her wallet in her backpack and ran out to meet her friends. Harper's mom drove a large, brand-new white van that was so clean it seemed to sparkle, and Izzy always felt a tinge of jealousy that Harper's family seemed to have the best of everything. Izzy never liked when it was her own mom's turn to drive the girls because her car was old and rundown and made a funny noise every time it started.

The Shopping Trip (cont.)

"Izzy, look at my new purse," Bailey said as she handed a small, sparkly pink plaid satchel over to Izzy.

Izzy gazed at it longingly and felt her face grow red with embarrassment because she had grabbed her backpack and didn't have a new purse too. "It's so cute," Izzy murmured as she handed the purse back to Bailey.

Harper's mom pulled into the mall parking lot and dropped the girls off at the entrance. "I am going to run some errands, but I expect you to meet me right here in two hours," Harper's mom said.

"We know, Mom! Thank you!" Harper called as she jumped out of the van. The girls linked arms and strolled into the mall.

"Let's get a treat first!" Bailey said, and they headed straight for the food court. The girls carefully looked at all the selections before deciding on frozen yogurt.

Izzy felt her face grow hot as she tried to add up the total in her head. It needed to be less than four dollars. She breathed a sigh of relief after Harper ordered hers and the clerk said, "Your total is three dollars and fifty cents."

Before Izzy ordered, she paused and thought about her dad's comment about spending wisely. But she figured that frozen yogurt was something that she could afford. The girls ate their treats and talked and laughed. Izzy's embarrassment about money disappeared as she wandered through the stores watching Harper and Bailey stop to make a few purchases.

The last store the girls checked out was a new jewelry store that sold beaded necklaces and bracelets. "I have an idea!" Harper exclaimed. "Let's all get matching bracelets, and we can call them best-friend bracelets.

"Oh, that's such a great idea," Bailey squealed, and they started comparing all the different bracelet styles.

Izzy felt a sense of dread as she felt her face burn with embarrassment. How would she pay for a bracelet? She didn't want to tell her friends that she didn't have enough money. Bailey handed her a pink and green crystal beaded bracelet. "I think this one is perfect for you," Bailey said with a smile.

Izzy held the tiny bracelet in her hand. It was perfect, and she loved it. "You're right," Izzy agreed.

Bailey and Harper bought their bracelets, but Izzy just stood holding hers. "Hey, I want to look at a few more things, and I will meet you out front," Izzy said nervously. The girls nodded and headed for the door as Izzy stared at the bracelet in her hand. The only thing she could think about was quietly sliding the tiny bracelet into her backpack and walking out. She had never stolen anything before, but it seemed as if it would be easy, and she felt too embarrassed to tell her friends the truth.

Should Izzy steal the bracelet?

Making Choices

Choice 1-Yes

Izzy felt her heart pounding in her chest and her face flaming red. She felt sweaty and uncomfortable, but she couldn't bear the humiliation of leaving the store without the bracelet. She bent over and pretended to tie her shoe and slipped the bracelet into the side pocket of her backpack. Then, she slid her arms through the backpack and quickly headed toward the door. She opened the shop door and grinned as she exited to meet Harper and Bailey.

As Izzy crossed through the door, the store alarm beeped loudly. "Oh no," Izzy thought as she turned around and looked back at the store. The clerk motioned for Izzy to return to the store. A security guard was suddenly at her side and escorted Izzy to the back of the store to question her.

Izzy confessed to taking the bracelet and handed it to the store clerk. The security guard said she needed to stay until they contacted her parents. Izzy felt the tears stream down her face. She was even more embarrassed now that she had to tell her parents what she had done.

Harper and Bailey were standing inside the store wide-eyed. Izzy just looked at her feet and said that her parents would be coming to get her. Her friends looked confused as they nodded silently and turned to leave. As Izzy waited for her parents to arrive, she realized that she should have just been honest with her friends. The embarrassment of being caught stealing and of not telling the truth was infinitely worse.

Choice 2-No

Izzy stopped and thought about her choices. She realized that while telling her friends that she couldn't afford the bracelet was embarrassing, stealing the bracelet would be worse. She placed the bracelet back on the rack and headed out of the store. Harper and Bailey were smiling as she approached, and Izzy instantly felt the hot flush of embarrassment on her face. "Where's your bracelet?" Bailey inquired.

"I was too embarrassed to tell you that my dad lost his job, and I don't get an allowance anymore, and I couldn't afford it," Izzy mumbled as tears slid down her face.

Harper gave Izzy a hug and said, "You don't have to be embarrassed about that. My parents didn't have jobs for a long time when I was little, and we lived with my grandparents."

Izzy wiped away her tears and replied, "I never knew that. I always feel embarrassed that we don't have as much money as your family does."

Bailey smiled at her. "Everyone has things they are embarrassed about, but it usually only matters to them. Remember that time Trevor teased me for having so many freckles? I was so embarrassed, but now I love them. They make me feel like me!"

Harper laughed, took off her shoe, and pointed to her foot. "I was born without a little toe! I used to be too embarrassed to wear sandals, but it's no big deal to me anymore. Oh, and remember that time I spilled my soda all over my clothes at the movie theater? I was so embarrassed, but now I think it's funny!"

Izzy laughed. "Thank you for being so supportive," she said as she hugged her best friends.

"Give me one second," cried Bailey as she ran into the shop. Minutes later, she returned with the pink and green bracelet. "Best friends forever," she said as she handed the bracelet to Izzy. They linked arms and headed out of the mall.

What Do You Think?

Choice 1

1 Why did Izzy steal the bracelet instead of just telling her friends the truth?

2 Do you think Harper and Bailey would have cared that Izzy didn't have any money?

3 How do you think Harper and Bailey felt when they saw that Izzy stole the bracelet?

4 What did Izzy learn about embarrassment?

Choice 2

1 Why did Izzy choose to not steal the bracelet?

2 Do you think Izzy was glad she made that choice?

3 How do you think Izzy felt after hearing about Harper and Bailey's embarrassing moments?

4 What did Izzy learn about friendship?

What Would You Do?

1 Have you ever been in an embarrassing moment? How do you feel about it now?

_____

_____

_____

_____

_____

2 How do you feel when you see someone else do something embarrassing?

_____

_____

_____

_____

_____

3 List one or more things you can do to feel better when you are feeling embarrassed.

_____

_____

_____

_____

_____

My Emotions: Embarrassment

Think about Izzy's story. Write about an experience you had when you felt embarrassed and what you have learned that could have made it feel better.

Understanding the Emotion: Worry

Summary

In this unit, students will read a story about a boy named Kevin who has to stay home and quarantine after a family trip. He struggles with worrying thoughts about his loved ones getting sick. Once the quarantine ends, Kevin has to make a choice about returning to the things he once loved, like swimming, or staying home because of his worry.

Class Discussion

Spend a few minutes discussing the social-emotional vocabulary for this unit. Write the word *worried* on the board. Ask students to define the word for you, then write their responses on the board. If time permits, have students share their prior knowledge and experience with the class regarding this emotion.

Remind students that feeling worried is an emotion we have all felt before. Worry is a little different than being afraid. Worry is feeling concerned that something could happen. We might worry that someone in our family might get sick if it's flu season. We might worry about getting a good grade on a test. When we worry, we tend to get stuck thinking about the bad things that could happen, instead of the good things.

Tell students that they will be reading a story about a boy who worries about his family getting sick during a virus outbreak. He has to make a choice to overcome his worry and return to his life or to stay home. Read the story (pages 66–67) aloud or distribute copies of the story to students to read on their own. Have students choose an ending (page 68) either as a group or individually. (See page 4 for additional ideas for working with the stories and endings.)

Coping Skill Activity

Tell students that when we worry, it is mostly just thoughts in our head that keep bugging us. A great way to calm these worrying thoughts is with yoga. When we practice yoga, we are connecting our minds to the movement of our bodies. This mind-body connection allows students to focus on the present and to eliminate those negative thoughts from their minds. Here is a quick yoga sequence to help students build concentration and focus:

1. Have students stand with their feet together and stretch their arms overhead while inhaling and gazing up to the sky.
2. Tell students to exhale as they fold forward. Have them sway back and forth as they release any tension.
3. Lastly, have students sweep their arms up as they return to the first pose, but this time, have them lift one foot and try to balance.

After going through the sequence, ask students how they feel. What were they thinking of as they were going through each pose? The goal is to have a clear, calm mind! (See page 77 for a bonus poster illustrating this yoga sequence.)

Personal Application

Have students come together as a whole group or in small groups to answer the discussion questions verbally. To conclude the unit, assign the written-response questions and the journal prompt as a way for students to relate the story to their own understanding of being worried and times they have felt this emotion in their lives.

Quarantine Days

"We're finally home!" Kevin said with an exhausted sigh, as he dragged in his heavy suitcase and collapsed on the hallway floor. His little sister Gloria giggled and collapsed next to him.

"Kids, get up," their mom laughed, "or I might run you over with my suitcase."

"What is this? Some sort of hallway party?" their dad joked as he carried in the last of the family's travel bags. They had just spent two weeks visiting family for their yearly summer trip across the country and had driven for days to get back home.

Kevin carried his suitcase to his room to unpack and then helped his little sister unpack hers. That night, he curled up into the comfort of his own bed and relaxed. As much as he enjoyed their family trips, he loved being home. They had spent days swimming in the lake, camping in the woods, and playing card games together as a family. Kevin looked forward to the trip every year, especially because he got to see all his cousins. But the familiarity of home always felt so good.

The next morning, the phone rang early as Kevin was still half asleep in bed. He heard his mom answer, and her voice drifted through the walls in a muffled hush. He couldn't hear what she was saying, but he was concerned about why someone would call so early in the morning.

Kevin rubbed his eyes groggily and stumbled sleepily into the kitchen just as his mom was hanging up the phone. She looked distressed as she walked over to Kevin and gave him a long hug. She then stared intently at his face and placed her hand on his forehead. "How are you feeling?" she asked in a determined voice.

"Fine, Mom," Kevin laughed, ducking away from her hand. "What's going on?"

Kevin's mom sat down at the kitchen table and sighed. "You know that virus that we heard about on the news while we were on vacation? Your uncle Daniel called to tell us that Grandpa Francis is in the hospital. He was feeling sick and tested positive for the virus. His doctor told him that everyone who has been in contact with Grandpa in the past few days needs to quarantine at home for two weeks."

Kevin looked confused and sat down at the table next to his mom. "Is Grandpa Francis going to be okay? What's a quarantine?"

His mom leaned over and patted his back reassuringly and replied, "The doctor expects him to recover in a few weeks. Quarantine just means that we need to stay home until we can prove that we aren't sick with the same virus as Grandpa. We cannot leave the house at all."

"Wait, we can't leave at all? But we just got home, and I haven't seen any of my friends this summer! I've missed all my swim team practices. I'm not sick at all, I promise. If I feel fine, I should be allowed to see my friends, right?" Kevin inquired.

His mom shook her head. "They said that we could spread the virus without even feeling sick, so we still need to stay home. I know it is frustrating, but we will make the best of it. Let's spend today making get-well cards for Grandpa Francis."

Quarantine Days (cont.)

Kevin helped his mom make breakfast while they waited for his dad and little sister to wake up. When Kevin's dad heard about the quarantine, he said he needed to report it to work because they would not let him come back into the office. His dad set up a computer in the living room and proclaimed it to be his office for the next two weeks.

Kevin and Gloria spent the day drawing pictures and coloring cards for Grandpa Francis. His mom cleaned out the kitchen pantry and made a list of the items they needed. Kevin looked at his mom and said nervously, "How will we get food?"

His mom showed him an app on her phone that that they could use to have groceries delivered. "I am taking all your food requests today and placing an order. But this food should last us for the next two weeks, so we will have to be smart about the things we choose," she said with a slight smile. "Don't just request ice cream!"

Gloria giggled and said, "Okay, I also request lots of chocolate chips!"

Kevin's family seemed to adapt to quarantine easily. But Kevin started having worrying thoughts that cycled through his head endlessly. He couldn't get them to stop. He started to feel anxious, and anytime that Gloria sneezed or coughed, he worried that she was sick with the virus. He called his Grandpa Francis every day just to make sure that he was starting to feel better. He felt dread when he watched the news and saw how many people were still getting infected with this virus. What if they left their house after quarantine and caught the virus then? Kevin began to think that his home was the only safe place. The worrying thoughts repeated endlessly in his mind, and his body felt so tense that he struggled to sleep at night.

Kevin's mom tried to entertain the family while they were stuck at home. She found a family yoga video, and she played it every night. At first, Kevin thought it was silly, but soon he realized that the deep breathing and rhythm and flow of the poses helped him feel better. They read lots of books, completed every puzzle in the house, and watched movies every night. They worked in the garden and even repainted the fence with some leftover paint they found in the garage.

Finally, their quarantine was over. They all wore face masks and drove to a clinic to make sure they tested negative before returning to society. The test was quick and easy, and they all were confirmed negative. "Yay," Gloria cheered. "I can go back to the park and see all my friends again!"

Kevin's dad was excited to return to the office and his mom said she was going shopping to replenish all the food that they needed in their pantry. Kevin's mom turned to him and said, "Kevin, you can finally see your friends and go back to swim team. Isn't there a swim meet tomorrow?"

But Kevin didn't feel ready to see his friends or go to the swim meet. The worried thoughts just kept spinning in his mind and his stomach felt anxious and swirly. What if someone at the swim meet was sick and infected them all?

Should Kevin go to the swim meet?

Making Choices

Choice 1—Yes

The next morning, Kevin's mom woke him early and reminded him of the swim meet. Kevin groaned and hugged his pillow tight. "What's wrong?" his mom asked with concern. "I thought you would be excited to go back to swimming."

Kevin sighed and decided to tell his mom about the worried thoughts in his head. After he explained the tense feelings and the fear about getting sick, she gave him a hug and reassured him that those worried thoughts were normal, and that he just needed to find a way to soothe them.

"Our town doesn't have anyone infected with the virus right now. Plus, the swim team is extremely cautious about keeping everyone safe. Everything is going to be fine, and you are going to love getting in that pool today!" his mom said with a grin. "Oh! I have an excellent idea. Come eat some breakfast and we can do the family yoga video before your swim meet."

Kevin smiled at his mom's enthusiasm, got out of bed, and followed her to the kitchen, eager to return to his real life again.

Choice 2—No

Kevin's worried thoughts kept him tossing and turning throughout the night, so when his mom came in early to wake him for the swim meet, he rolled over and moaned.

"Kevin, what's wrong? Are you not feeling well or are you nervous about the swim meet?" she asked with apprehension.

Kevin didn't want to express his concern to his mom, and he wasn't comfortable discussing the worried thoughts in his head, so he rolled over and said he didn't sleep well and wanted to stay home from the swim meet.

"But you haven't been in the pool all summer. Don't you miss swimming with your friends?" she asked.

Kevin's heart ached because he did miss swimming—and he also missed his friends, the competition, and the thrill of beating his past swim records. "I don't feel like I can swim today," he mumbled and pulled the covers over his head.

His mom agreed with a sigh and left him to rest. That afternoon, there was a knock on Kevin's bedroom door. "Come in," he called and smiled as his best friend Justin stormed in.

"I missed you so much this summer and was bummed that you didn't come to the swim meet today. We could have used you! Are you sick or something?" Justin asked excitedly, barely taking a breath between sentences.

Kevin smiled as soon as he saw Justin's face and heard his familiar voice. "No, I was feeling a little tired after staying home for so long."

"Well, get out of bed and come hang out! Let's go skateboarding before it gets dark," Justin cried. He grabbed Kevin's arm and pulled him out of his bed.

Kevin grinned and followed Justin out to the garage to grab his skateboard. As he skateboarded out of the garage and down the street, he realized that the worried thoughts had stopped spinning in his mind. He just needed to focus his mind on something else.

What Do You Think?

Choice 1

1. Why did talking about his worried thoughts help Kevin?

2. Do you think his mom was right about everything being safe?

3. How did yoga help Kevin?

4. How do you think Kevin will handle his worrying thoughts in the future?

Choice 2

1. Why did Kevin stay home from the swim meet?

2. Do you think talking about his worried feelings would help Kevin?

3. How did Kevin feel after talking with his friend Justin?

4. How did Kevin learn to calm his worried thoughts?

What Would You Do?

1 Is there something in particular that you worry about? Describe it.

_____

_____

_____

_____

2 Do you think worrying about viruses or natural disasters is a good thing? Why or why not?

_____

_____

_____

_____

_____

3 List one or more things you can do to calm your thoughts when you are feeling worried.

_____

_____

_____

_____

_____

My Emotions: Worry

Think about Kevin's worried thoughts about the virus. Have you ever worried about something that you couldn't control, such as a virus or a natural disaster? Write about your experience and what you have learned.

Journal Template

My Emotions _____

_____

_____

_____

_____

_____

_____

_____

_____

_____

_____

_____

_____

_____

_____

_____

_____

_____

_____

_____

_____

_____

Journal Template

Love Yourself!

"The things that make me different are the things that make me ME." — *A.A. Milne*

Draw a picture of yourself. Then, write about all the uniquely different and special things that make you YOU.

_____

_____

_____

Journal Template

Express Your Gratitude

The best way to calm feelings of jealousy, frustration, or sadness is to record your gratitude. Fill the gratitude jar below with the things you are thankful for in your life.

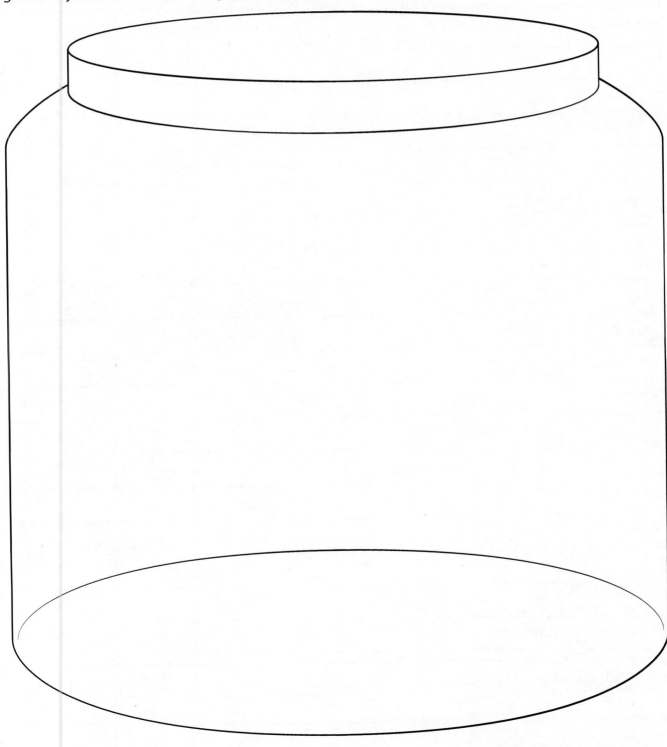

#8314 What Would YOU Do?

Journal Template

Mindful Meditation

Close your eyes for three minutes and pay attention to everything that is happening around you. Notice the sounds in the room. Think about how your body feels in your present environment—is it warm in the room or is there a cool breeze? Quiet your thoughts and listen to your own breathing. Increase the length of your inhales and slow down your exhales. Once your body feels calm and settled, write about your experience and the things you noticed while meditating.

_____

_____

_____

_____

_____

_____

_____

_____

_____

_____

_____

_____

_____

_____

_____

_____

_____

Journal Template

The Lightness of Laughter

"Laughter is the sun that drives winter from the human face." — *Victor Hugo*

Think about the quote. What do you think it means? How do you feel when you laugh? Write about a time that laughter helped you feel better in an emotional situation.

_____

_____

_____

_____

_____

_____

_____

_____

_____

_____

_____

_____

_____

_____

_____

_____

_____

_____

_____

_____

Journal Template

Conquering Fear

"You must never be fearful about what you are doing when it is right." — Rosa Parks

Rosa Parks is known as the first lady of civil rights. She fought against bus segregation and argued that black passengers should have the same rights to sit in whichever seat they choose. Think about her quote on fear. What does it mean to you? Write about a time you conquered your fear and stood up for something you believed was right.

_____

_____

_____

_____

_____

_____

_____

_____

_____

_____

_____

_____

_____

_____

_____

_____

_____

Yoga Sequence

Stand with your feet together and stretch your arms overhead while inhaling and gazing up to the sky.

Exhale as you fold forward. Sway back and forth to release any tension.

Sweep your arms up and return to the first pose, this time lifting one foot and trying to balance.

#8314 What Would YOU Do?

Tree Grounding

Plant your feet on the ground, shoulder width apart.

Breathe deep and hold your breath. Stiffen your whole body like a tree.

Exhale slowly, letting all the stiffness go.

Sway your body and arms gently like branches in the wind.

Belly Breathing

Sit on the floor with your legs crossed.

Place your hands on your belly and close your eyes.

Breathe in slowly and deeply to expand your belly.

Breathe out slowly to let your belly shrink.

Shape Breathing

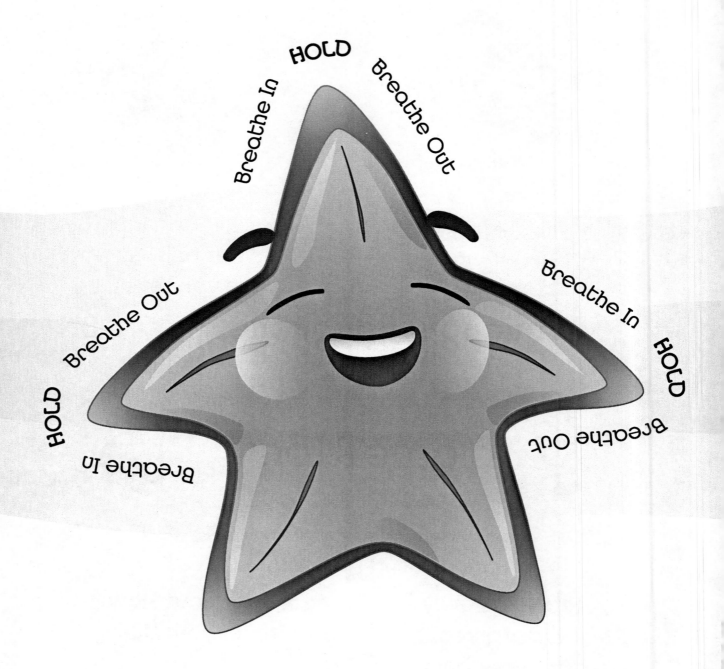